DISCIPLESHIP

Living in Union with Christ

Basic training in Christian doctrine
for pastors, evangelists, church leaders
and serious students

Produced and distributed by
AsiAfrica Ministries, Inc.
U.S.A.

© 2018 by Martin M. Davis. All rights reserved.

ABOUT THE AUTHOR

Rev. Martin M. Davis, Ph.D., is President of *AsiAfrica Ministries, Inc.*, a non-profit corporation promoting evangelism and biblical-theological education for church leaders in east Africa and south Asia. He holds a Doctorate in Theology from North-West University, Potchefstroom, South Africa, in conjunction with Greenwich School of Theology (UK). Dr. Davis is an Adjunct Faculty Member, Greenwich School of Theology/North-West University (Potchefstroom) South Africa. He is married to Sara W. Davis and has two stepdaughters and five grandchildren.

No part of this publication may be reproduced, stored in a retrieval system or transmitted in any way by any means—electronic, mechanical, photocopy, recording or otherwise—without the prior permission of the copyright holder, except as provided by USA copyright law.

Unless otherwise indicated, all Scripture quotations are taken from the Holy Bible, New Living Translation, copyright © 1996, 2004, 2007 by Tyndale House Foundation. Used by permission of Tyndale House Publishers, Inc., Carol Stream, Illinois 60188. All rights reserved. (British spelling used in this manual.)

Scripture quotations marked NIV are from THE HOLY BIBLE, NEW INTERNATIONAL VERSION®, NIV® Copyright © 1973, 1978, 1984, 2011 by Biblica, Inc.® Used by permission. All rights reserved worldwide.

Scripture quotations marked ERV are from "The Easy-to-Read Version of the Bible," published in 1989 by the World Bible Translation Centre.

Cover photo from Pixabay.com. Inside graphic courtesy of Pinterest.com.

TABLE OF CONTENTS

ABOUT THE AUTHOR i
Table of Contents ii
INTRODUCTION iv
CHAPTER 1: UNION WITH CHRIST 1
   Introduction.. 1
   A Reconciling Union 1
   The Wonderful Exchange 6
   Conclusion 9
CHAPTER 2: CHRIST IN OUR PLACE 10
   Introduction.. 10
   Jesus' Saving Life 10
   Re-living the Life of Adam 12
   Jesus Our High Priest 14
   A Cosmic Connection 18
   God Provides All He Requires 19
   The End of Religion 21
   Freedom and assurance in Jesus 22
   Summary..22
CHAPTER 3: THE COMMUNION OF THE SPIRIT 24
   Introduction..24
   The Coming of the Spirit 25
   The Communion of the Spirit...26
   Finding Ourselves in Jesus..27
   Summary..29
CHAPTER 4: DISCIPLESHIP (part 1) 30
   Introduction..30
   Faith 31
   Worship...36
      Worship as communion 37
      Christ-Centred Worship...38

- Church-Centred Worship ... 40
- Prayer ... 42
- Our Prayer Life ... 45
  - We pray in the name of Jesus ... 46
  - We pray by grace alone ... 46
  - We pray by faith alone ... 46
  - We pray in the Spirit ... 48
  - Into the presence of God ... 49
- Sacraments ... 50
  - Baptism ... 52
  - One Baptism ... 55
  - The Spirit Descends Upon Jesus ... 58
  - Summary ... 59
- The Lord's Supper (Holy Communion) ... 60
  - Remembrance ... 60
  - Participation ... 64
  - Response ... 65
  - Summary ... 67
- CHAPTER 5: DISCIPLESHIP (part 2) ... 68
  - Introduction ... 68
  - Holiness ... 69
    - Hidden With Christ ... 72
    - Become What You Are ... 75
    - Set Free in Jesus ... 77
  - Evangelism ... 78
  - The Logic of Grace ... 82
- Chapter 5: Summary ... 85

AsiAfrica Ministries, Inc.

INTRODUCTION

Welcome to our training manual, *Discipleship: Living in Union with Christ*, published by **AsiAfrica Ministries, Inc.** (USA). This manual is distributed free in PDF to pastors, evangelists, church leaders and serious students in Africa and south Asia.

The manuals, booklets and tracts produced, translated and distributed by AsiAfrica Ministries, Inc. clearly and boldly proclaim the good news of God's love for all humanity as revealed in Jesus Christ. We believe that your faith will be strengthened and your heart gladdened by the teachings you will discover in this manual.

This manual will challenge you to think of Jesus Christ in ways that you may find new, exciting and surprising. In the pages to follow, you will see that Jesus is bigger, better and more beautiful than many have dared to imagine. You will learn that everything needed for discipleship, or Christian living, is graciously given to us in Jesus.

This manual will challenge many readers to think of discipleship in a new way that is based on what Jesus has done for us, not on what we must do for Jesus. Unlike many books on discipleship, this manual does not outline a program to follow in order to live as disciples of Jesus Christ. This manual does not describe a series of steps to take in order to become disciples of Jesus, nor does it provide a list of rules we must follow for discipleship. As we shall learn, discipleship is not a program, a series of steps or a list of rules. **Discipleship** is the fruit of union with Christ through the communion of the Holy Spirit.

Because this manual presents the important matter of discipleship in a way that many will find not only new and exciting, but also liberating, we encourage you to take your time in reading it. Do not hurry. Do not merely read the words. Carefully study the teachings in this manual. Dwell on them, so that they become part of you. Ask the Holy Spirit to help you see Jesus in his fullness as the incarnate Saviour of the world.

While this manual was written originally for readers whose first language is not English, we have been happy to learn that its simple, non-technical language has proven helpful to American readers who seek a better understanding of the God who is "love" (John 4:8, 16).

AsiAfrica Ministries, Inc. is grateful to its partner ministries in Africa and south Asia who are helping us bring to their respective countries the good news of God's love for all, as revealed in Jesus Christ. We pray that this manual will be a blessing to you.

In memory of
Thomas F. Torrance
(1913-2007)

CHAPTER 1: UNION WITH CHRIST

INTRODUCTION

> **John 15:5:** "Yes, I am the vine; you are the branches. Those who remain in me, and I in them, will produce much fruit. For apart from me you can do nothing.
>
> **1 Peter 2:4, 5:** You are coming to Christ, who is the living cornerstone of God's temple. He was rejected by people, but he was chosen by God for great honour. 5 And you are living stones that God is building into his spiritual temple . . .
>
> **1 Corinthians 12:27**: All of you together are Christ's body, and each of you is a part of it.

"Union with Christ" is an important Christian doctrine. "Union with Christ" is an excellent way to describe the close, personal **relationship** believers have with Jesus Christ. The New Testament describes "union with Christ" in several ways. For example, we read that Jesus is the "Vine" and we are the "branches." Or, Jesus is the "living Cornerstone" of God's temple and we are "stones" in the Temple. Or, we are "parts," or "members," of Christ's body. These word pictures describe the close, personal **union** that believers share with Jesus. In this manual, we will learn that "discipleship," or "Christian living," is the fruit of our union with Christ. **Discipleship** is "living in union with Christ."

A RECONCILING UNION

To understand discipleship as "living in union with Christ," first we must understand clearly who Jesus Christ is. The New Testament says:

> **Matthew 1:23:** "Look! The virgin will conceive a child! She will give birth to a son, and they will call him Immanuel, which means 'God is with us.'

John 1:1-3, 14: In the beginning the Word already existed. The Word was with God, and the Word was God. ² He existed in the beginning with God. ³ God created everything through him, and nothing was created except through him. ⁴ The Word gave life to everything that was created, and his life brought light to everyone. ⁵ The light shines in the darkness, and the darkness can never extinguish it. ... ¹⁴ So the Word became human and made his home among us. He was full of unfailing love and faithfulness. And we have seen his glory, the glory of the Father's one and only Son.

Colossians 2:9: For in Christ lives all the fullness of God in a human body.

The person we know as Jesus of Nazareth is "Immanuel," or "God with us." Jesus is the eternal "Word" of God who became a human being and made his home among us. In Jesus, the fullness of God lives in a human body. When we speak of Jesus Christ, we speak of the one, unique person in human history who is both **fully God** and **fully human**.

Other New Testament teachings tell us more about who Jesus is:

Colossians 1:15-18: Christ is the visible image of the invisible God. He existed before anything was created and is supreme over all creation, ¹⁶ for through him God created everything in the heavenly realms and on earth. He made the things we can see and the things we cannot see—such as thrones, kingdoms, rulers, and authorities in the unseen world. Everything was created through him and for him. ¹⁷ He existed before anything else, and he holds all creation together.

Hebrews 1:1-3: Long ago God spoke many times and in many ways to our ancestors through the prophets. ² And now in these final days, he has spoken to us through his Son. God promised everything to the Son as an inheritance, and through the Son he created the universe. ³ The Son radiates

God's own glory and expresses the very character of God, and he sustains everything by the mighty power of his command.

John 1:3, 4: God created everything through him, and nothing was created except through him. 4 The Word gave life to everything that was created, and his life brought light to everyone.

Acts 17:28: For in him we live and move and exist. As some of your own poets have said, 'We are his offspring.'

These important scriptures deserve close attention and thought. Taken together, they reveal great truth about the person we know as Jesus Christ. According to these scriptures:

- Jesus is the visible image of the invisible God. Jesus radiates God's glory and expresses the character of God. Jesus is the "fullness" of God in human form.

- Jesus is the "Agent" of creation. That is, God created everything that exists through Jesus. The universe itself is the handiwork of Jesus Christ. Jesus made everything we can see and everything we cannot see.

- Jesus sustains and upholds everything by his mighty power. Jesus holds all creation together. Every tiny atom and every giant star is subject to Jesus. Every breath we take and every beat of our hearts is sustained by Jesus. Apart from Jesus, we cannot exist.

These scriptures show a close **connection** between Jesus and all creation ("the universe"). Jesus is the author, or agent, of creation. Jesus holds the entire creation together. Jesus sustains creation by his mighty power. The New Testament describes the connection between Jesus and all things in clear and simple terms: In Jesus, "we live and move and exist" (Acts 17:28).

Jesus, the Son of God, "was born as a human being" (Philippians 2:7) "in a body like we sinners have" (Romans 8:3). In other words, the Creator of all things became part of the creation! The Creator became a human being without ceasing to be God! Even as he took on human flesh in the womb of his mother Mary, the Eternal Son of God was upholding and sustaining the universe. What a mystery! What a cause for praise and worship! "In Jesus," the unique person who is both fully God and fully human, Creator and creation come together in **union**. "In Jesus," God and all humanity are joined together in intimate, personal **union**. Halleluiah!

The union of God and humanity in Jesus Christ is an **active**, living union. In other words, when God and humanity come together in the person we know as Jesus, something important happens! In Jesus, the world is **reconciled** to God. The New Testament says:

> **2 Corinthians 5:19:** For God was in Christ, **reconciling** the world to himself, no longer counting people's sins against them.
>
> **Colossians 1:19, 20:** For God in all his fullness was pleased to live in Christ, and through him God **reconciled** everything to himself.
>
> **1 Timothy 2:5:** There is one God and one Mediator who can **reconcile** God and humanity—the man Christ Jesus.

Jesus is the **Mediator** between God and humanity. A mediator **reconciles** two parties that are separated from each other. For example, a pastor may act as "mediator" between a husband and wife who are having problems in their marriage. The pastor's role is to bring the husband and wife together again in peace, love and harmony. In other words, the pastor seeks to **reconcile** the husband and wife to one another, so their marriage may be healed and

Discipleship: Living in Union with Christ

restored. In a similar way, Jesus is our Mediator. Jesus brings God and humanity together in love, peace and harmony. Humanity was separated from God because of sin (Isaiah 59:2). But Jesus **heals** our separation from God. Jesus **restores** us to right relationship with the Father. In Jesus, who is both fully God and fully human, the world is **reconciled** to God.

A "mediator" brings together people who are separated from each other.

Jesus is the Mediator between God and humanity.

(Courtesy ncworkercomp.com)

Let us think *carefully* about this very important matter. Jesus is the fully divine Son of God. Jesus is also fully human (John 1:14), born of a woman (Galatians 4:4) in a body like we sinners have (Roman 8:3). When the holy God and sinful humanity come together in the person we know as Jesus, the universe is forever **changed**! Sinful human beings are forever **changed**! The Eternal Son of God—the one who upholds and sustains the universe—brings his purity and holiness to bear upon the sinful human flesh he took from his mother Mary, and he **heals** it of its sinful corruption and decay. He **cleanses** it of the stain of Adam's sin. He **restores** it to right relationship with his Father in heaven. In short, Jesus makes our humanity **new**!

In Jesus, God and sinful humanity are forever joined together in reconciling union. *In Jesus*, we have peace with God (Romans 5:1). *In Jesus*, we are **new creations** (2 Corinthians 5:17).

> In Jesus the world is reconciled to God.

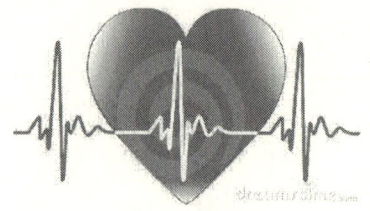

In Jesus, God and all humanity are joined in reconciling union. This is the beating heart of the Gospel.

(Courtesy of Dreamstime.com)

In Jesus, there is a bond between God and all humanity that cannot be broken. This is the beating heart of the Christian gospel. In Jesus, all humanity is joined to its Creator in intimate, personal **union**. Whether we know it or not, whether we believe it or not, *every human being* is connected to Jesus and sustained by him, for, in Jesus, we live and move and exist. In Jesus, all things are reconciled to God. In Jesus, God and humanity come together in peace and harmony, for Jesus **is** the union of God and sinful humanity.

We must be clear about this point! "Reconciliation" is not simply a saving "work" that Jesus does for us. Rather, reconciliation is the person of **Jesus** himself **at work** for us and for our salvation. In the person we know as Jesus of Nazareth, the one who is fully God and fully human, Creator and creation come together in saving, reconciling **union**. In Jesus, sinful humanity is joined to its Creator and healed and made **new**. Therefore, we must boldly proclaim to the world that Jesus **is** reconciliation between God and humanity. Jesus **is** the union of God and sinful humanity. Jesus **is** salvation! Praise God!

THE WONDERFUL EXCHANGE

In union with Christ, all that belongs to Jesus becomes ours! The Fathers of the early Church had a simple way to describe how we receive the blessings of our union with Christ. They said, *"Jesus became what we are, so that we can become what he is."* We find this teaching in the New Testament:

Discipleship: Living in Union with Christ

> **2 Corinthians 8:9**: You know the generous grace of our Lord Jesus Christ. Though he was rich, yet for your sakes he became poor, so that by his poverty he could make you rich.
>
> **2 Corinthians 5:21:** For God made Christ, who never sinned, to be the offering for our sin, so that we could be made right with God through Christ.
>
> **Philippians 2:6-8:** Though he was God, he did not think of equality with God as something to cling to. Instead, he gave up his divine privileges; he took the humble position of a slave and was born as a human being. When he appeared in human form, he humbled himself in obedience to God and died a criminal's death on a cross.

According to these scriptures, the eternal Son of God gave up the riches and splendour of heaven and became poor, so that we might become rich in the grace of God. Jesus exchanged the divine privileges of heaven for the humble position of slave and was born a human being, so that he might free us from the slavery of sin, death and the devil. Jesus became the offering for our sin, so that we can be "made right" with God.

In these scriptures, we see Jesus "exchanging" the glory and riches of heaven for our weakness and poverty in order to make us right with God. Bible teachers call this the **"wonderful exchange."** An example from ordinary life will help us to understand this important doctrine. If you want to buy fruit from a roadside seller, you give her money. In return, she gives you fruit. In other words, an "exchange" takes place. You give her money. She gives you food to eat. In the same way, Jesus makes a "wonderful exchange" with us. In "exchange" for our poverty, Jesus gives us his riches. In "exchange" for our weakness, Jesus gives us his strength. In "exchange" for our "wrong-ness," Jesus gives us his "right-ness." In "exchange" for our guilt, Jesus gives us his innocence. In "exchange" for our sinfulness, Jesus gives us his holiness. In "exchange" for our mortality, Jesus gives us his immortality. In "exchange" for our separation from God, Jesus includes us in his fellowship with the Father. In short, in the "wonderful exchange," Jesus takes our place so that we may have his place. Jesus becomes what we are, so that we may become what he is. In the "wonderful exchange," *all that Jesus is becomes ours.*

> **THE WONDERFUL EXCHANGE**
>
> Jesus takes our poverty and gives us his riches.
>
> In exchange for our guilt, Jesus gives us his innocence.
>
> In exchange for our sinfulness, Jesus gives us his holiness.
>
> In exchange for our "wrong-ness," Jesus gives us his "right-ness."
>
> Jesus takes all that is ours in order to give us all that is his.

Like reconciliation, it is important to understand that the "wonderful exchange" is not simply a "work" that Jesus does. Rather, the "wonderful exchange" is the Eternal Word of God "at work." The Eternal Word of God comes down from heaven and becomes a human being (John 1:14). The Eternal Word takes the sinful flesh of Adam from the womb of Mary and brings his purity and holiness to bear upon it, cleansing the stain of Adam's sin and healing our sinful humanity of its corruption, disease and decay. In Jesus, the new Adam, all humanity is made **new**. In Jesus, we are no longer slaves to sin, death and the devil. In Jesus, we are no longer stained by Adam's sin. In Jesus, we are healed, cleansed and restored to right relationship with the Father. In Jesus, we are new creations (2 Corinthians 5:17). Therefore, the "wonderful exchange" is an "atoning" ("saving") exchange that makes all humanity "at-one" with God.

CONCLUSION

Jesus **is** reconciliation between God and humanity. The reconciliation embodied in the person of Jesus Christ echoes across the universe, bringing all things into right relationship with God. In the wonderful exchange, Jesus takes all that is ours in order to give us all that is his. In the wonderful exchange, every man, woman and child is brought into saving union with Christ. In Jesus, all humanity is made new. The heart of the Gospel of Jesus Christ is the good news that, in spite of our sin, **all humanity** is chosen for salvation in Jesus. No one can escape the love of God that is revealed in Jesus. Since every human being exists by the Word of God by whom all things were made and in whom all things are held together, every man, woman and child, whether they know it or not, is gathered up safely in the arms of Jesus.

We are all in the arms of Jesus. (Courtesy of Pinterest.com)

CHAPTER 2: CHRIST IN OUR PLACE

INTRODUCTION

The "wonderful exchange" between Christ's riches and our poverty is a **saving** exchange. The eternal Word of God (Jesus) takes our sinful humanity from the Virgin Mary and gives us his holiness in exchange. In union with Christ, we are **made right** with God (1 Corinthians 1:30).

> **CHRIST IN OUR PLACE**
>
> Jesus acts in our place throughout his entire life, offering perfect faith and obedience to the Father in our name.

The "wonderful exchange," however, does not happen in only a single moment of time. The "wonderful exchange" takes place *throughout Jesus' life*. As "Jesus grew in wisdom and in stature and in favour with God" (Luke 2:52), he brought his purity and holiness to bear upon every stage of human life. From birth to death and beyond, Jesus acted **in our place** and **on our behalf**, cleansing the stain of Adam's sin and healing us from the disease of sin.

JESUS' SAVING LIFE

Jesus came into the world to save sinners (1 Timothy 1:15). Jesus is the Lamb of God who takes away the sin of the world (John 1:29). The cross of Christ is the great symbol of God's love for everyone (Romans 5:8). On the cross, Jesus set us free from the power of sin, death and the devil and opened the way to the Father's house for everyone (Hebrews 2:14, 15; John 14:2). Christians rightly place great importance on Jesus' saving death on the cross, for it is the central event of our salvation.

Discipleship: Living in Union with Christ

Nevertheless, Jesus' does not save us only by his death! To the contrary, Jesus' sacrifice for our salvation began in Bethlehem, when he was born of the Virgin Mary in a dirty stable surrounded by farm animals. In other words, Jesus' sacrifice for our salvation begins with the **incarnation**, when the Eternal Word of God left heaven in order to take "the humble position of a slave" and to be "born as a human being" (Philippians 2:7). The Eternal Word of God, through whom all things were created and in whom we live and move and exist, became a human being, so that he could fulfil God's plan and purpose for humanity. From the moment of his birth, Jesus lived his entire life in our place and **in our name**, as a sacrificial offering **for us** and for our salvation. From the moment of his birth, Jesus began to pay the price for our salvation and to heal and cleanse every part of our sinful human lives. From the stable in Bethlehem to the cross at Golgotha and beyond, Jesus acted **in our place**, reconciling humanity to God and sanctifying ("making holy") every stage of human life. The whole life of Jesus Christ is a life of self-offering to the Father on behalf of the whole world, reaching its goal in the one great sacrifice of love and obedience on the cross. Jesus' life of self-offering is the one sacrifice that is acceptable to the Father **for all people** in all places and at all times.

> **HE WALKED IN OUR SHOES**
>
> According to an old wise saying, if you want to know what another person's life is like, you must walk a mile in their shoes.
>
> Jesus walked a mile in our shoes. Jesus put on the old shoes of our ancestor Adam and walked in them throughout his life, re-living the life of old Adam, undoing his sin and making everyone right with God.

Hebrews 10:10-14: For God's will was for us **to be made holy** by the sacrifice of the body of Jesus Christ, once for all time. ¹¹ Under the old covenant, the priest stands and ministers before the altar day after day, offering the same sacrifices again and again, which can never take away sins. ¹² But our High Priest offered himself to God as a single sacrifice for sins, good for all time. Then he sat down in the place of honour at God's right hand. ¹³ There he waits until his enemies are humbled and made a footstool under his feet. ¹⁴ For by that one offering he forever made perfect those who are being made holy.

The writer of the Book of Hebrews tells us clearly that we are made **holy** and perfect forever by the sacrifice of Jesus Christ. "Holiness" is a **gift** we receive by grace. Believers do not have to earn holiness by the works of religion. We are made holy by the sacrifice of Jesus Christ.

Bible teachers often use the word, "**sanctification**," to refer to the biblical teaching that we are "made holy" in Jesus. In other words, we are *sanctified*, or "made holy," by the sacrifice of Jesus Christ. Contrary to some evangelical teaching, however, sanctification is not a long, slow process in which we become more and more holy through personal moral effort. We are *already* holy in Jesus. In the "wonderful exchange," we receive *all* Christ's riches, including his holiness.

RE-LIVING THE LIFE OF ADAM

We can better understand how Jesus acts in our place by comparing Jesus and Adam. Adam was the first man. He was the "head" of the human race. When Adam disobeyed God in the Garden of Eden, he brought the curse of sin and death upon *everyone* (Genesis 3:17-19; Romans 5:12). Adam's sin

Discipleship: Living in Union with Christ

broke fellowship with God. Adam's sin separated humanity from its Creator.

Jesus is the "new Adam." Jesus is the "new Head" of the human race (Romans 5:12-21). According to Irenaeus, a great Christian leader of the Second Century, Jesus "re-lived" ("lived again") the life of Adam. Unlike "old Adam," who sinned and disobeyed God, Jesus, the "new Adam," lived his entire life in perfect faith and obedience to his Father in heaven. The New Testament says:

> **A "DO OVER"**
>
> Have you ever made a terrible mistake that hurt yourself and others and wished you could do it all over again and make it right?
>
> Adam made a terrible mistake. His sin hurt himself and everyone else. Adam brought misery and death to all humanity.
>
> But Jesus is the "new Adam." Jesus came to do it all over again and make it right. In Jesus, *everyone* is "made right" with God.

> **Romans 5:18, 19 (ERV):** So that one sin of Adam brought the punishment of death to all people. But in the same way, Christ did something so good that it **makes all people right with God**. And that brings them true life. ¹⁹ One man disobeyed God and many became sinners. But in the same way, one man obeyed God and many will be made right.

"Old Adam's" disobedience brought the curse of death upon everyone. "New Adam's" obedience brings "true life" and "makes all people right with God." The New Testament says:

> **Romans 5:11:** So now we can rejoice in our wonderful **new relationship** with God because our Lord Jesus Christ has made us friends of God.

Through his perfect faith and obedience, Jesus restored **friendship** between God and sinful humanity. Jesus **reconciled** ("brought together in peace") God and the world

(2 Corinthians 5:19; Colossians 1:20). By *re-living* ("living again") the life of Adam, Jesus heals and cleanses every stage of human life. Through his perfect faith and obedience, Jesus brings the sinful human mind, heart and will back into right relationship with the Father. In Jesus, in whom we live and move and exist (Acts 17:28), all humanity is restored to right relationship with God. All that was lost and broken in Adam is found and restored in Jesus.

JESUS OUR HIGH PRIEST

We can better understand how all humanity is included "in" Jesus' saving life by looking back to the most holy day in ancient Israel's sacred calendar. On the annual "Day of Atonement" (*Yom Kippur*), all Israel's worship, prayers, offerings, and sacrifices for the entire year were gathered together in one holy event (Leviticus 16).

At the most solemn moment of this annual holy day, the High Priest entered the Tabernacle ("tent of meeting"), into the sacred room known as the "Most Holy Place"—the dwelling place of God. On his shoulders the High Priest wore the names of the twelve tribes of Israel. On his chest he wore a beautiful ornament of twelve precious stones, representing the twelve tribes of Israel (Exodus 39:6, 14). The entire nation's worship, prayers and sacrifices were represented by this **one man**, the High Priest, who acted **in the place of** the people and **in their name**. When the High Priest entered the Most Holy Place, **all Israel** entered the Most Holy Place "in him." **Everyone** was included in his sacred act.

Discipleship: Living in Union with Christ

In the Most Holy Place was a sacred box containing holy objects from Israel's history (Exodus 25:10-22). The box was called the "Ark of the Covenant." On top of the box were two angels made of gold. The top, or lid, of the box was called the "atonement cover." The "atonement cover" was the place where God met with his people. God spoke from between the "cherubim" (angels; Exodus 25:22). As representative of the people, the High Priest sprinkled the blood of a goat onto the "atonement cover" in order to "cover," or "atone" for the sins of the entire nation.

The Ark of the Covenant was the "meeting place" between God and his people. The lid or cover was called the "atonement cover."

(Courtesy of Pinterest.com)

 In the New Testament, the apostle Paul refers to Jesus Christ as "the atonement cover" (Romans 3:25). Paul teaches us that Jesus is the one in whom God and humanity "meet." God speaks to us through Jesus, who sheds his blood as the "atonement" for our sins!

The High Priest was the blood relative of his people. He was their "kinsman." He stood before God in the Most Holy Place in brotherly **union** with his fellow Israelites. He was the "one" who represented the "many." He represented all the people, so that his sacred acts were done in their place and **in their name**. After sprinkling blood on the altar, the High Priest prayed *for* the people and confessed their sins. When the High Priest confessed the sins of the entire nation, God declared *all* Israel forgiven "in" the person of the High Priest.

The High Priest acts in place of the people and in their name, so that everyone's sins are forgiven.

(Courtesy of greatstoriesoftheBible.net)

As the "mediator" ("one who brings two parties together") between God and Israel, the High Priest represented God to the people, and he represented the people to God. The High Priest embodied a "**two-way**" **movement of grace**, flowing from heaven to earth and back again from earth to heaven. In the movement of grace from heaven to earth, the High Priest ministered to the people in the name of God. In the movement of grace from earth to heaven, the High Priest ministered to God in the name of the people. In the person of the High Priest, heaven and earth came together in a "two-way," but unified movement of grace.

In the New Testament, we learn that the sacred act of the High Priest in Israel pointed forward in time to the priestly ministry of Jesus Christ (Hebrews 3:14-18; 4:14-16; 5:1-10; 6:19, 20; 7:23-28; 8:1-6; 9:1-28; 10:1-11). In the person we know as Jesus, we see the two-way movement of grace from heaven to earth and back again from earth to heaven. As the Son of God, Jesus represents the Father to humanity. Jesus speaks in the Father's name (John 12:49; 14:24). Jesus does only the Father's work and will (John 5:19, 20; 6:38). Jesus shows us the Father's love (Romans 5:8). This is the movement of grace from heaven to earth. As the "son of man," born of a woman (Galatians 4:4), Jesus represents humanity to the Father. Jesus lives his life **for us**, offering

Discipleship: Living in Union with Christ

perfect faith and obedience to the Father in our name. Jesus dies on the cross to take away the sin of the world and bring us home to the Father (John 1:29; 2 Corinthians 5:19; John 14:2). This is the movement of grace from earth to heaven.

When Jesus ascended to heaven after his glorious resurrection from the dead, "he entered the Most Holy Place [in heaven] once for all time and secured our redemption forever" (Hebrews 9:12). As our "kinsman," Jesus stands before the Father in brotherly union with us. He is our High Priest—"made in every respect like us, his brothers and sisters" (Hebrews 2:17). He is one with all races, colours, tribes and nations. Upon his shoulders he bears our names, our needs, our hopes and our sorrows. He offers to the Father his perfect faith and obedience **in our name**. Therefore, we are loved, accepted and forgiven in Jesus' priestly offering of himself to the Father. **In Jesus**, we are holy and without fault in the eyes of God (Ephesians 1:4).

We can learn much about how Jesus acts in our place from the well-known story of David and Goliath. When the young shepherd boy, David, fought the Philistine giant, Goliath (1 Samuel 17), David represented the entire nation of Israel. David acted **in place of** all the people of Israel. He was their "kinsman." When David went into battle, all Israel went into battle "in him." In other words, *David was the nation of Israel.* He acted in the name of all the people. If David wins the battle, the Philistines become the slaves of the people of Israel. If David loses the battle, all the people of Israel become slaves of the Philistines (1 Samuel 17:9). Therefore, *whatever happened to David happened to everyone!* All Israel was included in David's act. In the same way, everyone is included "in Jesus." Like David, Jesus acts **in place of** everyone. Jesus acts in the name of all humanity. Jesus wins the battle against sin, death and the devil and everyone is set free "in Jesus." Jesus offers perfect faith and obedience to the Father and everyone is included in his self-offering to the God. Everyone is made right with God "in Jesus." Everyone is made holy "in Jesus." Everyone is loved, forgiven and accepted "in Jesus."

A Cosmic Connection

In Israel, the High Priest was the "kinsman," or blood relative, of the people. The High Priest acted for the people as "one of the people," so that *all* Israel could receive forgiveness of their sins. Our High Priest, Jesus Christ, however, acts *for us* in a far greater and more personal way, because there is a *cosmic* connection between Jesus and all humanity. Jesus is the Agent of creation and the Sustainer of the universe. He is the one through whom all things were created and who holds all things together (John 1:1-3, 14; Colossians 1:16, 17; Hebrews 1:1-3). Jesus is the one "in" whom "we live and move and exist" (Acts 17:28). In the person we know as Jesus, God and *creation* come together in saving **union**. In Jesus, God has reconciled the world to himself (2 Corinthians 5:19; Colossians 1:20). In Jesus, we are "at-one" with God.

Jesus is the perfect human response to God.
We share in Jesus' perfect response to God.
(Courtesy PresenterMedia)

All humanity is in "**union with Christ**." All humanity is included in Jesus' life of perfect faith and obedience. When Jesus was baptised in the Jordan River, *we* were baptised "in him." When Jesus defeated Satan's temptation in the desert, *we* defeated temptation "in him." In the Garden of Gethsemane, where Jesus offered the perfect prayer of obedience to the Father, *we* surrendered our wills to the

Discipleship: Living in Union with Christ

Father "in him." On the cross, where Jesus put to death the "old Adam," *we* were "crucified with Christ" (Galatians 2:20). *We* died with him (2 Corinthians 5:14), so that *we* are no longer included in the "wrong-ness" of Adam. Instead, we are included in the "right-ness" of Jesus Christ (Romans 5:12-19). When Jesus rose from the dead, *we* rose from the dead "in him." We were born again "in him" (Ephesians 2:4-5; Colossians 1:3; 1 Peter 1:3). When Jesus ascended to the right hand of the Father, *we* ascended "in him," where *we* are "seated" with him "in heavenly places" (Ephesians 2:6). Because Jesus, the son of man, lived the life of perfect faith and obedience in *our* place and in our name—the "One" for the "many"—God graciously accepts and receives *us* "in him."

 When Jesus rose from the dead on the first Easter morning, all humanity was **born again** in him (1 Peter 1:3). All believers, whether Evangelical, Pentecostal, Protestant, Roman Catholic or Orthodox are rightly called "born again" Christians. The "new birth" is not a personal religious "experience" that happens to some believers but not others. To the contrary, we were **all** born again two thousand years ago when Jesus rose from the grave.

GOD PROVIDES ALL HE REQUIRES

In Old Testament Israel, God gave the people a system of law, rituals and sacrifices to enable a sinful people to worship a holy God in the proper way. The system of law and ritual was represented by the High Priest. In a movement of grace from heaven to earth, the High Priest ministered to the people in the name of God. In a movement of grace from earth to heaven, the High Priest ministered to God in the name of the people. The High Priest was the mediator who stood between heaven and earth, bringing God and his people together in peace and fellowship.

Today, Jesus is our High Priest. But unlike the High Priest of Israel, Jesus does not stand between heaven and earth. In the person of Jesus, heaven and earth are **reconciled**. That is, "in Jesus," heaven and earth come together in a "two-way," unified movement of grace from heaven to earth and back again from earth to heaven. In the "downward" flow of grace (from heaven to earth), the Eternal Word of God comes down from heaven to become a human being (John 1:1-3, 14; Philippians 2:5-8). As a human being, made in every way like we are (Hebrews 2:17), Jesus reveals God's love **for us** by dying on the cross to take away our sins (Romans 5:8). Many evangelical Christians think of Jesus only in terms of this all-important, "downward" movement of grace.

> **Jesus reveals God's love *to us*.**
> **Jesus responds to God's love *for us*.**

But there is another movement of grace: the equally important "upward" flow of grace (from earth to heaven). In the upward flow of grace, Jesus, the son of Mary, offers the perfect human response to God's love **in our place**. Jesus offers perfect faith and obedience to the Father **in our name**. Because Jesus is the one through whom all things are created and in whom we live and move and exist, **all humanity** is included in the upward flow of grace from Jesus to our Father in heaven.

The **Gospel** is the "good news" about Jesus (Mark 1:1). The man we know as Jesus of Nazareth embodies the two-way movement of grace **in his person**. In Jesus, who is both fully God and fully human, divine revelation and human response to the Father come together in a single, unified movement of grace. As the divine Son of God, Jesus comes down from heaven to reveal the Father's love and to save us from sin, death and the devil. As the human son of Mary, Jesus offers the perfect response to the Father's love. In Jesus, everything needed for human salvation is complete. Halleluiah!

Because Jesus **is** the perfect human response to the Father's love and will, nothing remains to be done for our salvation. In Jesus, our loving Father graciously **provides all he requires**. Our salvation is not a task we must finish by moral effort. Our salvation is not a reward we must struggle to earn by religious "works." To the contrary, Jesus *is* our salvation. Jesus *is* the perfect human response to God's will. In Jesus, it is finished (John 19:30).

THE END OF RELIGION

Because God provides everything he requires in Jesus, **nothing** remains for us to do in order to please God or to gain divine favour. Therefore, Jesus is the end of religion. "Religion" is the attempt to please or appease a distant, demanding god through human effort. "Religion" says that God is angry and we must do something to satisfy his anger. "Religion" says that the saving work of Jesus Christ is *not* enough for our salvation. "Religion" demands that *we add* something to Jesus "unfinished" work. "Religion" lays a heavy load of rules, laws, expectations, customs and rituals on our shoulders that we must carry if we are to be saved.

> Jesus is the end of religion.

Contrary to religion's demand that we finish our own salvation, everything needed for our salvation is "fulfilled" and "finished" in Jesus (Matthew 5:17; John 19:30). When Jesus offers to the Father his life of perfect faith and obedience in our place, Jesus sets us free from the burden of religion. Against the impossible, shaming demands of religion, we have an "Advocate" with the Father, Jesus Christ, who atones for the sins of all the world (1 John 2:1-3). Because Jesus our High Priest stands in *for us*, we can be certain that when we fall short of the goal set by "religion," Jesus crosses the finish line *for us*. When we are filled with confusion, uncertainty and doubt, Jesus believes *for us*. When we do not know how to pray, Jesus prays *for us*. When we give in to temptation, Jesus overcomes temptation *for us*. When we fail to love our neighbours as ourselves, Jesus loves them *for us*. When we balk at religion's heavy demands, Jesus offers perfect praise, worship, and obedience to the Father *for us*. Because Jesus acts in our place and in our name, we need not rely on religious "works" to please God. Instead, we rely on Jesus!

Freedom and assurance in Jesus

Jesus Christ, our Elder Brother and High Priest, stands **in our place** in heaven, "as man," representing us to the Father and including us in his priestly offering of perfect faith and obedience. Because God provides everything he requires in Jesus, we may lay down the heavy burden of religion. Because God provides everything he requires in Jesus, we may lay down the burden of doubt and uncertainty, for we have assurance that everything needed for our salvation is finished in Jesus. Because God provides everything he requires in Jesus, we may lay down the burden of fear, so that we may rest in hope, assured that all God's riches are ours in Jesus.

Summary

Jesus lived his entire life **for us**. Jesus offered perfect faith and obedience to the Father in our name. Jesus "re-lived" the life of Adam. Adam sinned and brought death to all. Jesus did it over again and brought holiness and life to all. In union with Christ, we are pure and holy in the sight of God. Jesus is our High Priest. He represents the Father to us. Jesus represents us to the Father. When the Son of God took our humanity from the Virgin Mary, he united humanity to himself. All humanity is in union with Christ. All humanity is reconciled to God in Jesus. All humanity is included in Jesus' priestly offering to the Father. In Jesus, we are made right with God. Jesus reveals God's love for the world. Jesus responds to God's love on behalf of the world. Jesus puts an end to "religion." In Jesus, God provides everything needed for our salvation.

CHAPTER 3: THE COMMUNION OF THE SPIRIT

Introduction

In the previous pages, we learned that Jesus is the Agent of creation and the Sustainer of the universe. We learned that God and the universe are brought together in reconciling union in Jesus. We learned that the fellowship between God and sinful humanity is restored in Jesus. We see Jesus' life and death played out on a grand scale, on a stage as wide as the universe. We see the universal scope of the incarnation of Jesus Christ. We see that everyone belongs to Jesus, for he is our Creator, Sustainer and Saviour. In him, we live and move and exist.

Yet the grand scale and universal scope of salvation may seem distant and remote to each of us personally. The universal reach of the incarnation of Jesus Christ may seem quite distant from our village, town or city. It may all seem long ago and far away. Therefore, many questions may remain. For example: "How do I *personally* take part in all that Jesus does for all humanity?" "If everything needed for our salvation is finished in Jesus, what am I supposed to do?" "Since Jesus offered perfect faith and obedience to the Father in my place and in my name, where does my *personal* faith and obedience fit in?" "Is my faith important?" "Does my obedience matter?" "Is there a place *for me* in the grand scale and universal scope of reconciliation?"

In order to answer these important questions, we must first consider the ministry of the Holy Spirit. In the following pages, we shall learn that everything Jesus does **for us** is made real **in us** by the ministry of the Holy Spirit. Through the communion ('fellowship") of the Holy Spirit, whom we receive through a simple act of faith, we actively and personally **participate**, or "share," in Jesus' perfect response to the Father.

THE COMING OF THE SPIRIT

Forty days after Jesus rose from the grave, he returned to his Father in heaven. Ten days later, on the day of Pentecost, the Holy Spirit came upon the disciples with great power (Acts 2:1-4). When the Holy Spirit came at Pentecost, something **new** and important happened. For the first time in human history, the Holy Spirit was "poured out" on all people. The apostle Peter explained what happened:

> **Acts 2:16, 17:** (Peter said) "[W]hat you see was predicted long ago by the prophet Joel: 'In the last days,' God says, 'I will pour out my Spirit upon all people.'"

In Old Testament times, the Holy Spirit only came upon prophets and leaders like Moses and Elijah, men of God who had a special mission to God's people, Israel. In the incarnation of Jesus Christ, however, sinful humanity's relationship to God is forever *changed*. When the Son of God took sinful human flesh from the Virgin Mary, he healed and cleansed it. Jesus made our humanity new! In addition, Jesus restored the relationship between God and humanity that was broken by Adam's sin. In Jesus, God and humanity are reconciled (2 Corinthians 5:19; Colossians 1:20). In Jesus, we are forever united to God in a fellowship of love, harmony and peace. Therefore, the Holy Spirit

On the Day of Pentecost, the Holy Spirit was "poured out" on all people.

(Courtesy of Coloringhome.com)

can be poured out on all humanity, because we are made clean and new in Jesus and restored to right relationship with the Father.

When Peter preached at Pentecost, he told the people how to receive the Holy Spirit. The New Testament says:

> **Acts 2:37, 38:** Peter's words pierced their hearts, and they said to him and to the other apostles, "Brothers, what should we do?" **38** Peter replied, "Each of you must repent of your sins and turn to God, and be baptised in the name of Jesus Christ for the forgiveness of your sins. Then you will receive the gift of the Holy Spirit.

When Peter finished his great sermon, about three thousand people believed what Peter preached about Jesus (Acts 2:41). They were baptised and received the Holy Spirit.

At Pentecost, Jesus shared the Holy Spirit with humanity, so that humanity might share by the Spirit in Jesus' relationship with the Father.

THE COMMUNION OF THE SPIRIT

As on the Day of Pentecost, those who repent of their sins, turn to God and are baptised in Jesus' name receive the gift of the Holy Spirit. The Father and the Son send the Holy Spirit to live in our hearts, so we may experience and enjoy our union with Christ. The Holy Spirit opens our eyes, ears and hearts to the glorious truth that Jesus has claimed us as his own and united us to himself in unbreakable fellowship. In the communion ("fellowship") of the Holy Spirit, believers *actively, knowingly, willingly, thankfully* **participate** ("share") in our union with Christ. In other words, the riches and blessings we receive from Jesus in the "wonderful exchange" are "**personalised**," or made real **in us** by the Spirit. In the communion of the Holy Spirit, all that Jesus has done **for us** in his life of perfect faith and obedience becomes **ours** in a real, living and **personal** way. By the Spirit, the perfect faith and obedience that Jesus offered to the Father **for us** begins to take root **in us**. By the Spirit, we begin to bear the fruit of our union with Christ.

The Holy Spirit does not bring about a new union. Rather, the Spirit awakens us to the reality of our union with Christ.

FINDING OURSELVES IN JESUS

Jesus did not come down from heaven only to take away our sins. Jesus came to make us pure, holy and right with God, so that he could bring us into **communion** ("relationship," "fellowship") with the Father (John 17:3). We are created to participate ("share") in Jesus' relationship with the Father through the communion of the Holy Spirit.

Therefore, relationship lies at the heart of our humanity. Relationship is a basic part of what it means to be human. We do not exist as isolated individuals, alone and separated from one another. We find our "identities," or our "sense of self," in our relationships. In marriage, a man and a woman become husband and wife, two persons joined together in a single **union** (Genesis 2:24). The marriage union is characterised by mutual giving and receiving. Each partner's identity, or "sense of self," is moulded and shaped by the new union. Their children are also formed and shaped by the particular traits and habits of the family. As the children get older, they participate in the wider community, where again their identities are moulded and shaped by the larger social group. People in the Global South are familiar with this idea. In Africa and Asia, people live and move and exist as part of a community that includes family, clan and tribe. Each person's "identity," or "sense of self," is moulded and shaped by the community. Relationships with others play an important part in making each person who they are.

Union with Christ is an "identity-forming" **relationship**. When the Eternal Word of God united himself to humanity in the womb of the Virgin Mary, he began to cleanse and heal our sinful flesh in order to make it new. Throughout his life on earth, the Son of God re-made and re-shaped sinful humanity. He brought his purity and holiness to bear upon Adam's sinful flesh and healed and cleansed it. Jesus restored fellowship between God and humanity. Jesus brought us unto communion ("relationship") with the Father. In union with Christ, our identities as human beings are re-made and re-shaped. In union with Christ, we are "new creations" (2 Corinthians 5:17).

> **The ministry of the Spirit is to turn us away from self and self-interest, so that we may find our lives in Jesus and in his relationship with the Father.**

Through the communion of the Holy Spirit, our new identities in union with Christ are made real and active **in us**. Union with Christ through the communion of the Spirit is a living, active, **transforming** relationship. Through the communion of the Spirit, believers **personally** participate in Jesus' relationship with the Father. Like all relationships, union with Christ through the communion of the Spirit moulds and shapes us at the deepest levels of our being, not only making us who we are but also who we are becoming!

Jesus does not send the Spirit to tell us what to do. Jesus sends the Spirit to tell us who we are! We are not slaves who must work to please a harsh master. We are the dearly loved sons and daughters of God (Romans 8:15; 1 John 3:1).

Summary

On the Day of Pentecost, the Holy Spirit was poured out on all flesh. By faith in Jesus, expressed in repentance and baptism, we receive the Holy Spirit in a personal way, so that we may actively, knowingly, willingly, thankfully participate in Jesus' relationship with the Father. By the Spirit, all that Jesus does for us begins to take root in us. By the Spirit, we begin to bear the fruit of our union with Christ. In union with Christ through the communion of the Spirit, our identities are moulded and shaped, as we turn away from self to find our lives in Jesus and in his relationship with the Father.

CHAPTER 4: DISCIPLESHIP (PART 1)

INTRODUCTION

Discipleship, or Christian living, is the fruit of the "identity-forming" relationship we have in union with Christ through the communion of the Spirit. In union with Christ, we are re-shaped and re-made. In union with Christ, we are "new creations" (2 Corinthians 5:17). Through the communion of the Holy Spirit, we find the meaning of our lives not "in" ourselves but "out" of ourselves in union with Christ. In union with Christ through the communion of the Spirit, we enter relationship with "Abba, Father" (Galatians 4:6). As the adopted, beloved children of God (Romans 8:15, 16; 1 John 3:1), we participate in Jesus' relationship with the Father. As we shall learn in the following pages, discipleship is the process of **discovering** our new identities in Jesus.

> Discipleship is the process of discovering our new identities in Christ.

Before we continue, however, we must clearly understand that discipleship is *not* a list of duties we must perform or a series of steps we must take in order to lead godly lives. Discipleship is not the pursuit of holiness through moral effort and spiritual struggle. To the contrary, discipleship is not about anything *we* must do to achieve holiness.

> Discipleship is based on what Jesus has done for us, not on what we do for Jesus.

Discipleship is first and foremost about what Jesus has already done **for us** and *continues* to do **for us** as our Elder Brother and High Priest. Discipleship is the believer's active, knowing, willing, grateful **participation** in the Son's offering of perfect faith and obedience to the Father in our place and in our name.

Discipleship may be expressed in many ways. In this manual, we shall explore discipleship in relation to faith, worship, prayer, the sacraments, godly living ("holiness") and evangelism.

Faith

Faith is an important part of discipleship. Faith involves **belief, trust** and **action**. "Faith" is believing that something is true and then acting on that belief. "By faith," we confess, or acknowledge, Jesus as our Lord and Saviour. "By faith," we receive all the blessings that are ours in the "wonderful exchange" between Jesus' riches and our poverty. "By faith," we trust Jesus to provide all that is needed for our salvation. "By faith," we order our lives according to our new identities in union with Christ. "By faith," we join our Elder Brother Jesus at the Father's table, taking our places as the beloved children of God.

For the Christian believer, faith involves absolute trust and confidence in Jesus Christ, for he is the "Leader" of our faith. The New Testament says:

> **Hebrews 12:2a ERV:** We must never stop looking to Jesus. He is the leader of our faith, and he is the one who makes our faith complete.

Jesus is the "Leader" of our faith. Jesus offers perfect faith to the Father **in our name**. Jesus makes our faith complete because he gathers it up and includes it in his own perfect faith. Therefore, "faith" means much more than our personal faith "in" Jesus. Even more important than our own personal faith "in" Jesus is the faith **of** Jesus, who offers his perfect faith to the Father **in our place** and in our name.

The apostle Paul understood the importance of the **faith of Jesus**. We will use the King James Version of the Holy Bible to help us understand. Paul writes:

> **Galatians 2:20:** I am crucified with Christ: nevertheless I live; yet not I, but Christ liveth ["lives"] in me: and the life which I now live in the flesh I live by the **faith of the Son of God**, who loved me, and gave himself for me.

The apostle Paul saw himself as "crucified" with Christ. In other words, Paul had died to his own selfish demands and desires. He lived only for Christ. Paul was totally committed to the Lord Jesus Christ. He willingly suffered great hardship in the service of his Lord (2 Corinthians 11:23-28). Yet his commitment to Jesus was not based on his "personal faith." Instead, he lived his life by the "**faith of the Son of God**."

To better understand Paul's meaning, let us turn to the Old Testament to consider the "faithfulness of God" in relation to the people of Israel. God made a *covenant*, or "agreement," with Israel. God said, "I will be your God and you will be my people" (Exodus 6:7; Jeremiah 30:22). God's covenant with Israel was a covenant of **grace**. God's covenant did not depend upon the faith and obedience of the people, for God knew that Israel was a rebellious, "stiff-necked" people (Exodus 32:9). The covenant depended only on the **faithfulness of God.** God gave himself totally to his people in steadfast love and faithfulness. The Old Testament says:

> **Deuteronomy 7:9:** Understand, therefore, that the Lord your God is indeed God. He is the **faithful God** who keeps his covenant for a thousand generations and lavishes his unfailing love on those who love him and obey his commands.

In unfailing love and faithfulness, God gave himself to Israel. Despite the people's constant unfaithfulness and disobedience, God remained faithful. Like a mother who never forgets her nursing child, God never forgot Israel (Isaiah 49:15, 16). Therefore, Israel's covenant relationship with God did not depend on the peoples' faith. It depended on **God's faithfulness** to them!

In a similar way, our covenant relationship with God does not depend upon our own "personal faith." Rather, our covenant relationship with God depends upon the **faithfulness of the Son of God,** who loves us and gave himself for us (Galatians 2:20 KJV). The Old Testament idea of the "faithfulness of God" takes human form in the person of Jesus. Jesus is the living proof of God's love for this sinful world (Romans 5:8). Jesus is the living proof that God will not abandon his world, for he sent his Son to save the world (John 3:16). In Jesus, we see the Old Testament idea of the **"faithfulness of God"** coming to life in a person. In Jesus, we see God's faithfulness and trustworthiness in action. Jesus embodies the faithfulness and trustworthiness of God. The apostle Paul writes:

> **2 Corinthians 1:19, 20:** For Jesus Christ, the Son of God, does not waver between "Yes" and "No." He is the one whom Silas, Timothy, and I preached to you, and as God's ultimate "Yes," he always does what he says. [20] For all of God's promises have been fulfilled in Christ with a resounding "Yes!" And through Christ, our "Amen" (which means "Yes") ascends to God for his glory.

Jesus Christ is God's "Yes" to humanity. In a movement of grace from heaven to earth, all God's promises are fulfilled in Jesus. At the same time, Jesus is humanity's "yes" to God! In a movement of grace from earth to heaven, Jesus offers the perfect human response of faith and obedience to the Father in the name of all humanity. Jesus is the True Believer. Jesus is the truly faithful human being. *"He is the leader of our faith, and he is the one who makes our faith complete"*

> By faith we receive the riches that are already ours in Christ.

(Hebrews 12:1, 2a). In union with Christ through the communion of the Spirit, our imperfect faith is gathered up and included in the perfect faith of Jesus. Therefore, our right standing with God is grounded on something much more solid and certain than our own "personal faith." Our right standing with God is grounded in, and supported by, the **faith of Jesus**.

Let us be clear about this important matter. Our standing with God depends solely upon the faith and obedience of Jesus—**prior to,** and apart from, our own personal decision of faith. Jesus is the one, great inclusive human being. All humanity is "in Jesus." Our union with Christ happened two thousand years ago, when the Eternal Son of God united sinful humanity to himself in the womb of the Virgin Mary. There are no "outsiders." There is no one who is not in union with Christ. There is no one who is not included in the perfect faith and obedience of Jesus. We do not become "insiders" by our personal decision of faith. Our personal decision of faith adds **nothing** to the finished work of Jesus Christ. Whether we know it or not, whether we recognise it or not, whether we appreciate it or not, we are all "insiders" by God's **grace** freely given us in Jesus. We are all **included** in the great circle of love that is the fellowship of the Father, Son and Holy Spirit.

Some readers will object, however, that so much emphasis on what Jesus has done **for us** in his own perfect faith and obedience neglects the believer's *personal* response of faith, devotion and piety. The faithfulness of Jesus, however, does not make our personal faith and obedience unnecessary or unimportant. To the contrary, through our personal response of faith, we actively, knowingly, willingly and

Discipleship: Living in Union with Christ

thankfully **participate** in God's riches given us in Jesus. Without "personal" faith, there can be no true knowledge and recognition of the riches freely given us in Jesus. Without faith, we cannot receive the great gift God has given us in Jesus. Without faith, there can be no thanksgiving and praise for all God has done for us in Jesus. Without faith, there can be no repentance and newness of life. Therefore, our personal faith is necessary to **recognise**, **appreciate** and **receive** all the riches that are ours in Jesus. While our personal faith does not move us from the "outside" of grace to the "inside," our faith allows us to see the joyous truth that we were *always* on the "inside," whether we knew it or not! Praise God!

In regard to the personal response of faith, devotion and piety, we are each like a small child who eagerly wants to help his older brother in the vineyard yet is unable to reach the ripe fruit hanging overhead. The child laughs with delight, however, as his bigger, stronger brother lifts him up, so that he too can pluck the fruit from the branches. The small child is enabled to "help" with the harvest because he is supported by his older, stronger brother. Like the happy child, we too are lifted up by the Holy Spirit, where we may **participate**, or "take part," in our Elder Brother's priestly work.

By faith, through the communion of the Spirit, we participate in the Son's priestly offering to the Father.

Thus, the perfect faith and obedience of Jesus Christ, offered on behalf of all and in place of all, does not negate or diminish the importance of our personal responses to God. To the contrary, our Elder Brother's faith and obedience makes our personal

> **"THE RESPONSE"**
>
> Jesus *is* the perfect human response to God.
>
> The believer's personal faith is a "response" to "The Response" that Jesus has already made *for us.*

response possible. Jesus' priestly offering to the Father enables, strengthens and supports our personal and communal responses of faith, devotion and piety. Jesus himself is the perfect human response to the will of God. Our "personal faith" is **a response to his Response**. In other words, "by faith," we respond to what Jesus has already done **for us**. In Jesus, our "Amen" to God ascends to heaven to the glory of God (2 Corinthians 1:20), as our personal and communal worship is lifted up by the Holy Spirit and included in Jesus' own priestly self-offering to the Father.

When our faith is weak, or when we have doubts, we can trust Jesus to believe for us! Jesus includes us in his perfect faith and obedience. With the apostle Paul, we say, "I, yet not I but Jesus." Therefore, let us lay our burden at the feet of our Elder Brother. Halleluiah!

WORSHIP

Worship is an important part of discipleship, or Christian living. Worship is our response of praise and thanksgiving to God for all he has done for us in Jesus. The New Testament says:

> **Romans 12:1:** And so, dear brothers and sisters, I plead with you to give your bodies to God **because of all he has done for you**. Let them be a living and holy sacrifice—the kind he will find acceptable. This is truly the way to worship him.

Discipleship: Living in Union with Christ

In worship, we offer **ourselves** to God as "a living and holy sacrifice." We give ourselves to God in mind, body and spirit. In worship, we offer our prayers in humble expectation. We lift our voices in songs of praise. We lift our hands in thanksgiving.

Worship as communion

Why is worship important? Why do Christians come together each week to worship God? Is worship a duty we must perform to please God? Do we gather simply to learn useful lessons for daily life? Do we gather to learn how to gain wealth and prosperity? Or do we gather together for reasons that are more important than the cares of daily life or the increase of riches? To answer these questions, we must first return to the basic questions of our faith: Who is God? Who is Jesus Christ? Who is the Holy Spirit? Why did God create us? What is the purpose of our lives?

"God" is Father, Son and Holy Spirit—three equal, divine Persons who eternally exist as "One" in a **fellowship of love**. As John says, "God is love" (1 John 4:8, 16). The nature of love is *to reach out to another*. Love seeks **relationship** with another. In a gracious act of overflowing love, God created us to share his love with us. Because God loves us, God wants **to share himself** with us. God wants to enjoy relationship with us. God wants us to enjoy relationship with him. In short, we are created for communion ("fellowship"). God wants to be **our God**. God wants us to be **his people** (Exodus 6:7; Jeremiah 30:22; 2 Corinthians 6:16; Revelation 21:3).

> In worship, we enter into communion with God.
>
> Worship is the expression of our love for God.

Worship arises from the knowledge of "Who" God is and his loving purpose for humanity. When we understand "Who" God is and how much God loves us, we discover that we want to be in relationship with God. We want fellowship, or "communion," with God. We want to give ourselves to God, and we want to experience and enjoy God's self-giving to us in Jesus and the Holy Spirit. **Worship is an expression of our love for God.**

Worship is not a duty we must perform to please God. Worship is not a means to an end, such as health, wealth or prosperity. To the contrary, worship is a **response** to God's love, grace and goodness toward us, as revealed in Jesus. In worship, we enjoy communion with God. Through the ministry of the Holy Spirit, we share in the Son's fellowship with the Father. In worship, the community of faith is spiritually lifted up into the loving heart of the Holy Trinity.

The eternal Son of God did not come down from heaven only to save us from sin, death and the devil. The Son of God came to bring us into communion with our Father in heaven. God loves us. God wants fellowship with us. God wants us to enjoy fellowship with him.

Christ-Centred Worship

True Christian worship is **Christ-centred**, for there is only one who has authority to enter into the Most Holy Place in heaven. He is Jesus, our Elder Brother and High Priest. Jesus is the **Leader** of our worship. The New Testament says:

> **Hebrews 8:2:** [Jesus] "ministers in the heavenly Tabernacle ["tent of meeting"], the true place of worship that was built by the Lord and not by human hands."

Even now, Jesus ministers in the Most Holy Place in heaven. Christ-centred worship is **participating**, or "sharing," in

Jesus' High-Priestly ministry in the communion of the Holy Spirit. In worship, the community of faith is lifted up by the Spirit into Jesus' intimate fellowship with the Father. As a "royal priesthood" (1 Peter 2:9), we gather in worship to participate in Jesus' priestly offering of praise to God and intercession for the world. As a royal priesthood, we offer praise, worship and thanksgiving to the Father in the name of Jesus. As a royal priesthood, we bear the grief and sorrows of the world. We pray for all humanity in the name of Jesus, asking the Father to remember those who are suffering, who are in sorrow, or who are in need. When the community of faith gathers as the royal priesthood of God, worshipping and praying in the name of Jesus, we remind the world that this is Jesus' world. He is Lord, both by right of creation and redemption.

In worship, we offer ourselves to the Father "in the name of Jesus Christ." We can worship only "in Jesus' name," because he is the Mediator between God and humanity. Jesus, our High Priest, made the perfect offering to God in our place and in our name. By the sacrifice of Jesus Christ, we are made **holy** for all time in the eyes of God. The New Testament says:

> **Hebrews 10:10-14:** For God's will was **for us to be made holy** by the sacrifice of the body of Jesus Christ, once for all time. [11] Under the old covenant, the priest stands and ministers before the altar day after day, offering the same sacrifices again and again, which can never take away sins. [12] But our High Priest [Jesus] offered himself to God as a single sacrifice for sins, good for all time. Then he sat down in the place of honour at God's right hand. [13] There he waits until his enemies are humbled and made a footstool under his feet. [14] For by that one offering **he forever made perfect** those who are being made holy.

In the "wonderful exchange" between Jesus' riches and our poverty, Jesus takes our unworthy praise, prayers and offerings and cleanses and *sanctifies* them ("makes them holy"). Then he presents them to the Father "without a spot or wrinkle or any other blemish" (Ephesians 5:27). In the "wonderful exchange," Jesus makes our worship and praises his own, and he makes his worship and praises our own. Jesus, our High Priest, stands in the Most Holy Place, bearing our names upon his shoulders, offering perfect worship to the Father in our name. Therefore, worship is "all of grace." It is God's **gift** to us. The upward movement of grace (from earth to heaven) is provided **for us** in Jesus. By grace, we may share in the Son's fellowship with the Father in the communion of the Spirit. Christ-centred worship is *not* about us and what we do for Jesus. **Christ-centred worship is about Jesus and what he does for us**. He is the High Priest. He offers his perfect faith and obedience to the Father **in our name**.

 If we think of worship as something we must do to please God, we fall back into the bondage of religion. Christ-centred worship focuses on what Jesus does for us, not on what we do for Jesus. Worship is not about what we do in Jesus' name. Worship is about what Jesus' does in our name. In the communion of the Holy Spirit, we share in all that Jesus does **for us** with joy, peace and confidence.

Church-Centred Worship

We can better understand "Christ-centred" worship by comparing it with "church-centred" worship. "Church-centred" worship is common in many "mega-churches," where congregations number in the thousands. "Church-centred" worship is not about what Jesus does for us. It is about what **we** do for God. "Church-centred" worship

Discipleship: Living in Union with Christ

focuses on *our response* to God: our faith, our decision, our repentance, our obedience. In "church-centred" worship, we are the priests (not Jesus!), offering our worship and praise to God "in Jesus' name," hoping that God will hear and approve.

In contrast to "Christ-centred" worship, "church-centred" worship often focuses on the pastor (not Jesus!). The pastor performs, struts and parades, shouting "halleluiah" and "amen," while the congregation watches with approval. Many see the pastor (not Jesus!) as the mediator between God and the people, because he or she is thought to be more holy and closer to God than others. Because the pastor is the star of the show, the congregation is reduced to an audience watching a carefully staged performance. The priesthood of Jesus Christ is nowhere to be found, because the pastor takes centre stage and leaves Jesus waiting in the wings.

In "church-centred" worship, the pastor is the centre of attention.

(Courtesy Joe Cassada blog)

"Church-centred" worship does not do justice to the fullness of grace embodied in the person of Jesus Christ. "Church-centred" worship rightly appreciates the downward movement of grace (from heaven to earth) that focuses on the cross of Christ, but it ignores the upward movement of grace (from earth to heaven) that Jesus offers to the Father in our place and in our name. Contrary to "church-centred" worship, Jesus (not the pastor!) is our Mediator and High Priest. Jesus (not the pastor!) offers perfect worship, praise and prayer to the Father **in our place** and on our behalf. Jesus (not the pastor!) includes our imperfect worship, praise and prayers in his own and offers them to the Father without stain or blemish **in our name**.

The Christian Church must return to Trinitarian, Christ-centred worship. Pastors and evangelists must preach the good news about Jesus (Mark 1:1). They must teach the fullness of grace embodied in Jesus, in both its downward and upward movements. Like John the Baptist, pastors and evangelists must become *less* so that Jesus can become *more* (John 3:30). Believers must trust Jesus not only to take away our sins (downward movement of grace) but also to include us in his perfect worship, praise and prayer (upward movement of grace). Jesus is the Leader of our worship. He is the High Priest. He is the focus of our faith. He is the Finisher of our salvation. In short, Jesus is the centre of it all.

Prayer

Like worship, prayer is an important part of discipleship. Jesus spent much time in prayer (Hebrews 5:7). Jesus rose early in the morning and went alone to a quiet place to pray (Mark 1:35). Sometimes, Jesus prayed all night (Luke 6:12). Throughout his life, Jesus did only his Father's will (John 6:38). Prayer was an important way for Jesus to nurture his close relationship with his heavenly Father.

Through prayer, we, too, nurture our relationship with our Father in heaven. In prayer, we talk to our heavenly Father, confessing our sins, asking for forgiveness, praying for others, expressing our needs and hopes and asking for guidance. The New Testament tells us to pray without ceasing and to give God thanks in all things (1 Thessalonians 5:17-18). The Holy Bible teaches us to pray about everything:

Philippians 4:6: Do not worry about anything; instead, **pray about everything**. Tell God what you need, and thank him for all he has done.

Sometimes, however, we do not know how to pray. We may be confused and uncertain what to pray about. We wonder if our prayers are pleasing to God. We wonder if God hears our prayers. But thanks be to God! We do not pray alone, for **Jesus**, our Elder Brother and High Priest, **prays for us**. Jesus includes our prayers in his own priestly offering to the Father. The New Testament says:

> **Hebrews 7:23-26:** There were many priests under the old system, for death prevented them from remaining in office. 24 But because Jesus lives forever, his priesthood lasts forever. 25 Therefore he is able, once and forever, to save those who come to God through him. **He lives forever to intercede with God on their behalf.** 26 He is the kind of high priest we need because he is holy and blameless, unstained by sin. He has been set apart from sinners and has been given the highest place of honour in heaven.

Jesus "intercedes" for us. He is our "Intercessor." An "intercessor" speaks on behalf of another. Jesus, our High Priest, speaks *for us*. He "intercedes" with God on our behalf.

> **INTERCESSOR**
>
> Jesus is our "Intercessor." Jesus speaks *for us*.

The writer of the Book of Hebrews uses the priestly language of Old Testament Israel to interpret the ministry of Jesus, even in regard to **prayer**. On the Day of Atonement (Leviticus 16) the prayers and offerings of all the people of Israel were gathered up in one man, the High Priest, who stood in for the people, acting in their place and in their name. When the High Priest prayed in the Most Holy Place, the people waited outside the

Tabernacle ("tent of meeting"), praying along with him. The prayers of the High Priest and the prayers of the people rose to heaven together in a single fragrant offering to God.

In the same way, Jesus, our High Priest, stands in the Most Holy Place in heaven, offering prayers to the Father in our name. In the "wonderful exchange," Jesus gathers up our imperfect prayers, cleanses them, and includes them with his own prayers, so that they rise together as a single fragrant offering to our Father in heaven (Psalm 141:2; Revelation 5:8). As in worship, prayer is "all of grace." The upward movement of mediation is graciously provided **for us** in Jesus, who stands in our place and prays on our behalf. Therefore, when we pray, we depend completely on Jesus' prayers to the Father in our name.

Jesus takes our prayers and includes them in his own prayers.

(Courtesy weclipart.com)

When we turn away from our own imperfect prayers in order to rest in Jesus' priestly prayer for us, we are truly praying "in Jesus' name." In the communion of the Spirit, Jesus puts his prayer on our unclean lips, so that we may pray with him, through him, and in his name and be received by our Father in Jesus (Hebrews 5:7). In union with Christ through the communion of the spirit, there is no division between Jesus' prayer and our prayers, for they are one and the same. Jesus gathers our prayers with his prayers and includes them in his priestly offering to the Father.

Discipleship: Living in Union with Christ

Jesus our High Priest is at the Father's side, speaking on our behalf. The New Testament says:

> **Romans 8:34 ERV:** Who can say that God's people are guilty? No one! Christ Jesus died for us, but that is not all. He was also raised from death. And now he is at God's right side, **speaking to him for us**.

Even in our prayer life, Jesus, our High Priest and "Intercessor," takes our place and speaks to God **for us**. In all our prayers, whether we pray alone or with others, we come before God in such a way that **Jesus prays for us**. Jesus gathers up our prayers with his own prayers and presents them to the Father as a fragrant offering.

 We can apply Galatians 2:20 to prayer: "We pray, yet it is not we who pray but Christ who prays for us and in us. And the prayers we now offer in the flesh, we offer by the faithfulness of the Son of God, who loved us and gave himself for us." Even in prayer, we follow Paul's principle: "I, yet not I but Christ."

OUR PRAYER LIFE[1]

With the understanding that Jesus includes our prayers with his own prayers to the Father, there are five important points to remember about our prayer life:

- We pray in the name of Jesus
- We pray by grace alone
- We pray by faith alone
- We pray in the Spirit
- We enter into the presence of God

---

[1] For much of the material in this section, I am indebted to the late James B. Torrance, Professor Emeritus of Systematic Theology, University of Aberdeen, Scotland.

We pray in the name of Jesus

We can only pray in the name of Jesus because of what Jesus has already done for us. Jesus lived a life of perfect faith and obedience **in our place** and on our behalf. In the "wonderful exchange," Jesus took our guilt to the cross and bore the judgement on sin that we deserve. Jesus "became sin for us, so that we could be made right with God" (2 Corinthians 5:21). In the "wonderful exchange," Jesus takes our desires, wishes, hopes and fears, makes them his own and includes them in his own prayers to the Father. Therefore, we can joyfully pray "in the name of Jesus" because of what he has already done for us and continues to do for us today as our High Priest.

We pray by grace alone

We do not know how to pray as we ought, so Jesus, our Elder Brother, prays for us, with us, and in us. Like worship, prayer is a gift of **grace**. The Father graciously gives his Son to stand in for us, even in our prayer life. Grace is the expression of the Father's heart, who includes us in Jesus' prayer life and draws us into holy communion ("fellowship") by his Spirit. Grace is **unconditional.** There are no demands or requirements that we must meet in order to be blessed by God's goodness and kindness. Prayer is not a duty we must perform in order to please God. Rather, prayer is a joyful **response** to God's goodness toward us, for, in his unfailing love and grace, God has given all we need for salvation in his Son Jesus.

We pray by faith alone

"By faith," we look away from ourselves in prayer toward God our Father, trusting our Lord Jesus to intercede for us and to express our prayers in a manner well-pleasing to the

Father. In prayer, we abandon ourselves to the ministry of Jesus Christ. We surrender our wills to the Father, as expressed in a beautiful way in the "Prayer of Abandonment" by Charles de Foucauld:

> "Father, I abandon myself into your hands: Do with me what you will. Whatever you will do, I will thank you. Let only your will be done in me, As in all your creatures. And I will ask nothing else, my Lord.
>
> Into your hands I commend my spirit: I give it to you with all the love of my heart, For I love you Lord, and so need to give myself, To surrender myself into your hands, With a trust beyond all measure, Because you are my Father."

We find the spirit of faith and abandonment in the prayer of the young peasant girl, Mary, when the angel Gabriel announced that she would give birth to the Son of God. Mary said, "I am the Lord's servant. May everything you have said about me come true" (Luke 1:38). Mary, the Virgin mother of Jesus, surrendered her life to God's will. She let go of self-interest in order to become an empty vessel in the hands of God.

In the same way, Jesus completely surrendered his will to the Father in the Garden of Gethsemane on the night before he was crucified. Jesus prayed, "Father, if you are willing, please take this cup of suffering away from me. Yet I want your will to be done, not mine" (Luke 22:42). Jesus surrendered his own will to the Father's will. Jesus abandoned himself, so that the divine plan for the salvation of humanity could be fulfilled.

Like Mary and Jesus, we abandon ourselves in prayer to God's will. We place ourselves in the Father's loving hands, trusting him and believing that his love for us is faithful and true.

We pray in the Spirit

Romans 8:26, 27: Also, the Spirit helps us. We are very weak, but the Spirit helps us with our weakness. We do not know how to pray as we should, but the Spirit himself speaks to God for us. He begs God for us, speaking to him with feelings too deep for words. ²⁷ God already knows our deepest thoughts. And he understands what the Spirit is saying, because the Spirit speaks for his people in the way that agrees with what God wants.

Trinitarian Prayer

Prayer is the gift of participating through the **Spirit** in the **Son's** prayers to the **Father**.

Christian prayer is **Trinitarian** ("involving the Holy Trinity"): In union with **Christ** through the communion of the **Holy Spirit**, our prayers ascend to heaven as a fragrant offering to our loving **Father**. In short, we pray in the **Spirit** through the **Son** to the **Father**. In the communion of the Holy Spirit, we participate by prayer in the Son's relationship with the Father. The Doctrine of the Holy Trinity is the foundation for understanding Christian worship and prayer.

As Christians, we know we should pray. Yet we do not know how to pray as we ought. We try to prayer, but we fail. Sometimes we pray with wrong motives, seeking only things that give us pleasure (James 4:3). But God loves us. Despite our own imperfect prayers, God wants to draw us into fellowship with himself. Therefore, Jesus prays in our name and on our behalf—praying for us and in us and with us—sending his Spirit into our hearts so that we may cry out "Abba, Father" (Romans 8:15; Galatians 4:6). The Holy Spirit lifts us up into the fellowship of the Father and Son,

Discipleship: Living in Union with Christ

where Jesus draws us into his prayer life and includes us in his priestly offering to the Father.

In our prayer lives, as in our daily lives, we look away from ourselves to Jesus, our Elder Brother and High Priest. By faith we abandon ourselves in prayer in order to be led by the Holy Spirit into the Son's communion with the Father. We trust Jesus, who is at the right hand of the Father, including our prayers in his prayers and interceding on our behalf and in our name.

Into the presence of God

Through the communion of the Holy Spirit, in whom we are lifted in spirit to heaven, our High Priest, Jesus Christ, leads us into the Most Holy Place, into the presence of the Father Almighty. The Holy Bible says:

> **Hebrews 10:19-22:** And so, dear brothers and sisters, we can boldly enter heaven's Most Holy Place because of the blood of Jesus. 20 By his death, Jesus opened a new and life-giving way through the curtain into the Most Holy Place. 21 And since we have a great High Priest who rules over God's house, 22 let us go right into the presence of God with sincere hearts fully trusting him. For our guilty consciences have been sprinkled with Christ's blood to make us clean, and our bodies have been washed with pure water.

When Jesus died on the cross, the heavy curtain in the Temple that hid the Most Holy Place from view was torn in half from top to bottom (Matthew 27:51). By his death on the cross, "Jesus opened a new and life-giving

Jesus, our High Priest, takes us by the hand and leads us to the Father.

(Baptistandreflector.org))

way through the curtain into the Most Holy Place" in heaven, so that we may "go right into the presence of God" with trusting hearts, and in full confidence, that we will be received by our loving Father.

Through the ministry of Jesus Christ, our High Priest, we sinful human beings may enter the Most Holy Place, into the presence of the Most Holy God. We do not need to "make ourselves holy" in order to enter into the presence of God. In Jesus, we are already "holy and without fault" (Ephesian 1:3, 4). We do not need sacrifices, ceremonial washings, magic or strange rituals to make us worthy to enter into the presence of God, for *Jesus has already made us holy* (John 17:17-19). Jesus made us holy when he took our sinful flesh from the Virgin Mary and healed and cleansed it of the stain of Adam's sin. Jesus made us holy when he rose from the grave in bodily form (Luke 24:38-41) and ascended into heaven, taking our own humanity into the Most Holy Place, into the presence of God the Father. The New Testament says:

> **Hebrews 4:16:** So let us come boldly to the throne of our gracious God. There we will receive his mercy, and we will find grace to help us when we need it most.

We may pray with confidence, knowing that whenever we pray and wherever we pray, we are lifted by the Spirit to Jesus, who takes our prayers and offers them to the Father in our name. Therefore, let us pray always (1 Thessalonians 5:17), with faith, trust and confidence, for our heavenly Father is listening closely to the prayers of his beloved children.

SACRAMENTS

Evangelicals, Pentecostals and Protestants recognise two "sacraments": 1) baptism and 2) the Lord's Supper. While Roman Catholic Christians recognize other sacraments in

Discipleship: Living in Union with Christ

addition to these two, our focus in this manual will be on baptism and the Lord's Supper.

Sacraments are "signs" that point to important spiritual realities.

(CanStockPhoto)

A **sacrament** is a visible, physical "sign" that points beyond itself to a spiritual reality. When we travel to a distant village or city, we find signs along the road that point us in the right direction. The purpose of a sign is to show us the way to go. The sign itself is not the way. Rather, the sign points to the way. The sign points beyond itself to our journey's end. In a similar way, baptism and the Lord's Supper are visible, physical signs that point beyond themselves to important spiritual realities. The sacraments point to what God has done for us in Jesus and continues to do for us through his Spirit.

God graciously gives us the sacraments of baptism and the Lord's Supper as proper ways to respond to God's love and goodness toward us. The sacraments are not about what we do for God, however. The sacraments are about what God does **for us** in Jesus. The sacraments point us away from ourselves to Jesus. Through the sacraments of baptism and the Lord's Supper, we **participate**, or share, in Jesus's priestly offering of perfect faith and obedience to God. Through the sacraments, the worshipping community says "yes" to the complete and perfect "Yes" Jesus offers to the Father in our place and in our name. Baptism is a public sign of our once-and-for-all union with Christ through the communion of the Spirit. The Lord's Supper reminds us again and again that we are continually fed spiritually through our union with Christ. Both sacraments remind us that we find our lives outside ourselves in union with Christ through the communion of the Spirit.

Baptism

> **Matthew 28:18, 19:** Jesus came and told his disciples, "I have been given all authority in heaven and on earth. ¹⁹ Therefore, go and make disciples of all the nations, baptising them in the name of the Father and the Son and the Holy Spirit.

Jesus' own baptism in the Jordan River was Trinitarian.

(Courtesy of Pinterest.com)

What is the meaning of baptism? Why does our Lord Jesus command his disciples to baptise? What is the spiritual reality that baptism points to?

First, baptism by water is a "sign" of the one work of the Father, Son and Holy Spirit, who are bringing many sons and daughters into glory (Hebrews 2:10). We baptise in the Name of the Father, Son and Holy Spirit because the Church's mission to the world is grounded in the mission of the Son and Spirit, who are sent by the Father to bring many sons and daughters into the family of God.

When Jesus was baptised in the Jordan River (Matthew 3:13-17), his own baptism was **Trinitarian** ("having to do with the Holy Trinity"). As the **Son** of God, Jesus received from the **Father** the baptism of the **Holy Spirit** in his own humanity, so that, "as man," he could stand in our place and act on our behalf, even in baptism. From beginning to end, the work of salvation is Trinitarian. The Father sends the Son and the Holy Spirit to bring us into the life, love and beauty of the Holy Trinity. Therefore, we baptise in the Name of the Father, Son and Holy Spirit.

Some churches baptise "in Jesus' name" only. If we baptise in Jesus' name only, however, we separate, or divide, the work of the Son from the work of the Father and the Holy Spirit. Separation or division is contrary to the nature of God. As "One God," the Father, Son and Holy Spirit work together in harmony, purpose and unity of will in order to bring many sons and daughters into glory. Therefore, we must follow Jesus' command and baptise in the Name of the Father, Son and Holy Spirit (Matthew 28:19).

Second, baptism by water is a "sign" of the covenant ("agreement") of grace in which our loving God freely claims us as his people. In the covenant of grace, God says, "I will be your God and you will be my people" (Exodus 6:7; Jeremiah 30:22). Baptism shows that we are God's people. We are his beloved children (1 John 3:1). We are members of the family of God. Baptism shows that we have a new Lord, whose name is Jesus. Baptism shows that we are saved from the kingdom of darkness and that we belong to the Kingdom of Light. Baptism shows that we are no longer under the rule of law but we are under the rule of grace. We are dead to sin and alive to God. Baptism shows that old things have passed away and all things are made new in Jesus.

Before the creation of the world, out of an abundance of love, God chose us to be his people (Ephesians 1:4). God's covenant of grace does not depend upon our personal faith, our "decision for Christ" or our obedience. If God's grace depended on us, then baptism would be a sign of what we do for God, not what God does for us. The good news is that God made a covenant of grace with us that was sealed with the blood of Christ two thousand years ago! Through the grace that is given to us in Jesus, God claims us as his own people. God calls us to respond to his grace and love by saying "yes" to Jesus and serving him as Lord.

Third, our baptism by water is a "sign" of Christ's baptism in blood. Christ spoke of his death on the cross as a "baptism" (Luke 12:50; Mark 10:38). Through Jesus' "baptism" on the cross, we are forgiven our sins and sanctified ("made holy"), because we are washed clean in the blood of the Lamb. The Holy Spirit seals the sacrifice of Christ in our hearts and calls us to share in Jesus' death and resurrection through a life of daily dying to self and rising with Christ.

Thus, baptism by water is a "sign" that points beyond itself toward important spiritual truth. Baptism is a sign of what God does **for us**. The "rite," or "ceremony," of baptism does not save us. We are saved *only* by the grace, goodness and mercy of God, as revealed in Jesus and the Holy Spirit. We are not washed clean of the stain of sin by the water of baptism. We are washed clean from sin only by the blood of Jesus. Salvation is "all of grace." Therefore, we do not baptise ourselves, for we are not the agents of our own salvation. Rather, we humbly **receive** baptism as a "sign" of our total, complete dependence upon God for our salvation. We receive baptism as a sign that we are not saved by our personal faith or obedience. Rather, we are saved only by the perfect faith and obedience of Jesus. Thus, we are baptised "out of ourselves" and "into Jesus." Baptism bears public witness to the fact that we are not our own (1 Corinthians 6:19, 20), for we belong to Jesus, who is our Lord and Saviour.

Discipleship: Living in Union with Christ

One Baptism

Ephesians 4:5: There is one Lord, one faith, **one baptism** ...

Jesus was baptised on our behalf and in our name.

(Courtesy of Pinterest.com)

Whether we are Evangelical, Pentecostal, Protestant, Roman Catholic or Orthodox, Christians believe in "one baptism." What does the New Testament mean when it speaks of "one baptism"?

"One baptism" refers primarily to Jesus' baptism **for us**. Jesus began his public ministry when he was baptised by John in the Jordan River. Many people came to John to confess their sins and to be baptised as a sign of repentance. Jesus was not a sinner, however (2 Corinthians 5:21; Hebrews 4:15). He did not need to confess his sins or to receive baptism as a sign of repentance. Jesus came into the world *to save sinners* (1 Timothy 1:15). By receiving John's baptism, Jesus identifies with sinners. Jesus puts himself **in the place of** sinners. Jesus bears **our** guilt and submits to God's judgement **for us**. As our Substitute and Representative, the divine Son of God receives baptism in his humanity on behalf of all humanity, in the place of all humanity and in the name of all humanity.

Thus, the **central truth** of baptism is found in Jesus himself. Jesus' entire life was a "baptism" **for us** and for our salvation. From the moment of his birth in a "body like the bodies we sinners have" (Romans 8:3), Jesus carried God's righteous verdict of "guilty" upon his own shoulders, as he marched to the cross in order to be baptised in blood to take away the sin of the world (John 1:29). Jesus bore our guilt once and for all—the one for the many—so that his baptism is our baptism, his death is our death, his burial is our burial and his resurrection to new life is our resurrection to new life (1 Peter 1:3). Our personal baptism is a public witness to our participation, or sharing, though the communion of the Spirit, in the "one," **all-inclusive** baptism of Jesus, worked out for us through the whole course of his life of perfect faith and obedience.

Baptism is the sacrament of the *reversal* of the sinfulness and corruption that humanity took from our ancestor, Adam. Just as Adam's disobedience was reversed, or "turned back," by Jesus' obedience, our sinful condition is reversed when Jesus takes our sinful humanity from the Virgin Mary and heals and cleanses every stage of human life throughout his life on earth. Therefore, holiness, purity and "right-ness" before God are not promises that we receive in the distant future. They are *already* ours in Jesus. Through union with Christ in the communion of the Spirit, we *already* share in the new humanity made clean, pure and holy by Jesus. We are born again through the life, death and resurrection of Jesus. We are personally "washed" in the water of baptism as a public sign that we are *already* new creations in Christ (2 Corinthians 5:17).

> **Baptism is the sacrament of the "wonderful exchange," where Jesus gives us his riches in exchange for our poverty.**

Baptism is the sacrament of the "wonderful exchange." In union with Christ, we share all Christ's benefits and blessings, so that all that belongs to Jesus is **ours**. Through Jesus' birth in a body like we sinners have, we are cleansed from the stain of Adam's sin and made members of a new humanity. Through his perfect faith and obedience unto death, we are forgiven our sins and made right with God. Through his resurrection we are set free from the power of

Discipleship: Living in Union with Christ

sin, death and the devil and are "born again" (1 Peter 1:3). Through his ascension to heaven, the way to the Father's house is opened wide for us (John 14:2; Hebrews 10:20). Through sharing his Spirit, we are made members of his "Body" and brought into the fellowship of the Holy Trinity. Finally, in union with Christ through the communion of the Spirit, we share in Christ's suffering by entering into a life of self-giving and service to others, as we take up our crosses daily and follow Jesus (Matthew 16:24).

 When Jesus rose from the grave, we were born again in him. We are new creations in Christ (2 Corinthians 5:17). Our new birth does not happen when we make a "personal decision" for Christ. Our new birth does not happen when we are baptised. Our new birth happened two thousand years ago when Jesus rose from the grave and made all things new. The New Testament shows the **connection** between the resurrection of Jesus Christ and our "new birth":

1 Peter 1:3: All praise to God, the Father of our Lord Jesus Christ. It is by his great mercy that we have been **born again**, because **God raised Jesus Christ** from the dead.

Many evangelical Christians believe that the "new birth" is a powerful, personal, spiritual *experience*. This experience is so powerful, they say, that one can never forget when it happened. They insist that only believers who have had this personal experience are "born again" Christians. The "new birth," however, is *not* a personal experience that only some believers enjoy. **All** believers, whether Evangelical, Pentecostal, Protestant, Catholic or Orthodox, are "born again" through the resurrection of Jesus Christ. We are **all** new creations in Christ!

The Spirit Descends Upon Jesus

When Jesus was baptised, the Holy Spirit descended from heaven like a dove (Matthew 3:16; Luke 3:22). The Spirit did not descend upon Jesus to make him holy, however, for Jesus is without sin (2 Corinthians 5:21; Hebrews 4:15). To the contrary, Jesus received the Holy Spirit **for us**. As our High Priest, Jesus received the baptism of the Spirit in **his humanity** in the name of all humanity.

The Holy Spirit descends upon Jesus at the Jordan River.

(Courtesy of Pinterest.com)

When the holy Son of God took our sinful flesh from the Virgin Mary, he cleansed it of sin and made it pure and holy. Because we live and move and exist in Jesus (Acts 17:28), and because Jesus is the one in whom all things consist (Colossians 1:17), everyone is gathered into the humanity of Jesus and cleansed of the stain of Adam's sin. The Spirit's descent upon the humanity of Jesus bears witness to the holiness and purity of humanity in union with Christ. Now that the Spirit has descended upon the humanity of Jesus, the Holy Spirit can be poured out on **all people** (Acts 2:16, 17).

Jesus was baptised in our place and in our name. Jesus was washed in the Jordan River **for us**. Jesus received the Holy Spirit **for us**. Today, Jesus continues to baptise believers with the Holy Spirit (Luke 3:16). Jesus sends the Spirit so that we may know and enjoy our union with him. Jesus sends the "Spirit of adoption," so that we may enter into Jesus' "family-fellowship" with the Father. Through the baptism of the Spirit, we know God as "Abba, Father," for the Spirit "testifies with our spirit that we are God's children" (Galatians 4:6; Romans 8:15, 16). Jesus sends the Spirit to gather believers together as members of Christ's "Body" (1 Corinthians 12:27). Jesus sends the Spirit to bring us together in fellowship, as the community of faith. Jesus sends the Spirit to build us up in love and to send us into the world with his message of hope. Therefore, we are baptised into the community of believers that worships the **Father**, in and through the **Son**, in the communion ("fellowship") of the **Spirit**.

Summary

In summary, baptism is a sign that points to important spiritual realities. First, baptism points to the one work of the Father, Son and Spirit in bringing us into glory. Second, baptism is a sign of the covenant of grace, wherein God graciously and lovingly claims us as his own people. Third, baptism is a sign of Christ's baptism in blood on the cross for us and for our salvation. Christians everywhere believe in "one baptism." This refers to Jesus' baptism **for us** in the Jordan River and to his baptism **of us** by the Holy Spirit. By "one baptism," the community of faith is gathered "into Christ," as members of Christ's own "Body" and sent into the world in hope.

Neither Jesus nor the writers of the New Testament give us specific instructions about baptism. They do not tell us how to baptise. They do not tell us how much water to use or how to apply it. They do not tell us the proper age for baptism. Jesus and the writers of the New Testament were not concerned about the ceremony itself. They were concerned about the spiritual reality to which baptism points. Today, Christians have different ideas about baptism. We do not all agree on the method of baptism or the proper age for baptism. Nevertheless, we all agree that baptism points to something beyond itself. The ceremony of baptism that is administered by the church points to the "one baptism" of Jesus Christ in the Jordan River, as well as his entire sacrificial life, death and resurrection for us and for our salvation. Believers must not argue and fight with one another about baptism. The world knows we are disciples of Jesus Christ because we love one another (John 13:35). We may disagree on the ceremony of baptism, but we must disagree in **love** for one another. If we fail to love one another by fighting and arguing about baptism, we destroy our witness and discredit the Gospel of Jesus Christ.

THE LORD'S SUPPER (HOLY COMMUNION)

Like baptism, the Lord's Supper, or Holy Communion, is a sign that points to Jesus. In the Lord's Supper, we **remember** the sacrifice Jesus made to take away the sin of the world. In the Lord's Supper, we **participate** ("share") in Jesus's priestly offering of perfect faith and obedience to God. In the Lord's Supper, we **respond** to God's love and goodness for us, as revealed in Jesus.

Remembrance

The Lord's Supper, or "Holy Communion," is an important part of discipleship. Gathered in peace, harmony and love, the people of God take bread and wine (or, juice) to **remember** the sacrifice that Jesus made to take away the sin of the whole world.

On the night before Jesus died on the cross, he shared a meal with his disciples. The Holy Bible says:

> **Matthew 26:26-28:** As they were eating, Jesus took some bread and blessed it. Then he broke it in pieces and gave it to the disciples, saying, "Take this and eat it, for this is my

body." And he took a cup of wine and gave thanks to God for it. He gave it to them and said, "Each of you drink from it, for this is my blood, which confirms the covenant ["agreement"] between God and his people. It is poured out as a sacrifice to forgive the sins of many."

Jesus knew he would die on the cross the next day. Therefore, he needed a way to teach his disciples about the meaning of his death. Jesus could have preached a sermon. Instead, he gave his disciples a **meal**!

Jesus ate his final meal with his disciples during the festival of **Passover**. During this sacred festival, everyone remembered the time long ago when their ancestors were slaves in Egypt. They told the story about the night when the angel of death went throughout Egypt and all the first-born of Egypt died. God told his people to sacrifice a lamb and put the blood of the lamb on the doorposts of their homes. When the angel of death saw the blood of the lamb, he would "pass over" their homes and everyone inside would be saved from death (*see* Exodus, Chapter 12).

Following the night of "Passover," God rescued the people of Israel from slavery in Egypt. God guided his people safely through the waters of the Red Sea, where God destroyed the army of Pharaoh, the evil king of Egypt. God led his people to Mount Sinai, where he remembered the **covenant**, or "agreement," he made with their ancestor Abraham. God said to the people of Israel: "I will be your God, and you will be my people." God gave the people the Law, including the Ten Commandments, so they would know how to live as the people of God. With God's Law as their guide, the people of Israel were to be a "light to the nations," so that other nations could learn to live the right way. God told the people to make a special tent, or "Tabernacle," where God could live among his people. Finally, God led his people to the land that he promised to Abraham and his descendants.

During the time of Jesus, the festival of Passover held great meaning for the people of Israel. Like their ancestors, who were ruled by the evil king of Egypt, the people were ruled by the powerful pagan nation, Rome. Therefore, Passover represented escape from the rule of evil kings. Passover represented freedom from slavery. Passover represented **forgiveness** of sins and **freedom** from the curse of disobedience. Passover represented the time of God's special protection for his people. Passover represented the time when God remembered his **covenant** ("agreement") with his people and came to dwell among them in the holy Tabernacle. Passover represented freedom, hope and a bright future when God would dwell again with his people.

Jesus chose this special time to go to Jerusalem to give his life for the sins of the world. All the great events associated with **Passover** would now be associated with **Jesus' death** on the cross. Jesus died on the cross to defeat Satan, the evil "ruler of this world." Jesus died to bring forgiveness of sins, and to rescue *everyone* from the slavery of sin and death. Jesus died so that God could once again dwell with his people when the Spirit was poured out on all flesh (Acts 2:17, 33).

During the final Passover meal with his disciples, Jesus took **bread.** He blessed it in prayer to his Father in heaven. Then he broke it. He said to the disciples, "Take this and eat it, for this is my body." Then Jesus took a cup of **wine** and gave thanks to his Father. He said, "Each of you drink from it, for this is my blood, which confirms the covenant between God and his people." The bread and wine represent the body and blood of our Saviour Jesus Christ. Jesus gives his **body** and **blood** in sacrifice to take away the sin of the world, so that

everyone may receive forgiveness of sins and be set free from the slavery of sin, death and the devil.

Today, when we take the bread and wine of the Lord's Supper, we **remember** the sacrifice that Jesus made to take away the sin of the world. In humble thanksgiving, we remember his suffering and death. We remember his body broken for us and his blood shed for our salvation. We remember that we are called to share in the suffering of Christ and to take up the cross and follow him.

> **When we take the bread and wine as the family of God, Jesus is present in a special, intimate way!**

But the Lord's Supper is much more than remembering an important event that happened long ago. The same Jesus who delivered us from sin, death and the devil two thousand years ago is with us today. Jesus rose from the grave. He is no longer bound by time or place. The Risen Christ is with us **here and now** in the bread and wine. In a mysterious way known only to God, the resurrected Jesus is spiritually **present** among us, feeding us in the bread and wine to strengthen our spirits, to build us up in love and to send us into the world with his message of hope. In the Lord's Supper, the past becomes alive today, as we remember that **we** are the people for whom Jesus died and rose again. **We** are the people whose sins Jesus bore on the cross and washed away with his blood. **We** are the people to whom God says, "I shall be your God and you shall be my people." **We** are the people who know Jesus as Lord and God as "Abba, Father." **We** are the people whose sorrows, suffering and grief Jesus bears in his heart, as he cries out to the Father in our name. In the Lord's Supper, we remember that we are who we are today because of what Jesus did **for us** then.

Participation

In addition to remembrance, the Lord's Supper is an important means of **participation**, or "taking part," in the High-Priestly ministry of our Elder Brother, Jesus Christ. When we take the bread and wine (juice) of the Lord's Supper, the Holy Spirit **lifts up our hearts** into the Most Holy Place in heaven, where we participate in Jesus' priestly offering to the Father. Jesus, our High Priest, is the Leader of our worship (Hebrews 12:2). In his humanity, Jesus presents **himself** to the Father **in our name**. In his humanity, in a body like we sinners have, Jesus offers the one true sacrifice that is pleasing to God. As our High Priest, Jesus offers the perfect human response to grace (from earth to heaven), so that all God requires is complete in Jesus. Our Elder Brother Jesus gathers **us** up and includes **us** in his perfect response and presents **us** to the Father as God's beloved children—holy, blameless and without a single fault.

> In the Lord's Supper, we participate in the worship of the heavenly sanctuary, which Jesus offers to the Father in our name.

We stretch out empty hands to receive the bread and wine.

(Courtesy of Pinterest.com)

The Lord's Supper helps us to understand how we participate in all that Jesus does **for us**. The Lord's Supper is the regular, on-going "sign" of our participation, or "sharing," in the perfect response of faith and obedience that Jesus offers to the Father in our place and in our name. The Lord's Supper is an act of worship, prayer and thanksgiving. In the communion of the Spirit, we participate in the worship, prayer and thanksgiving that Jesus offers to the Father. We come to the Lord's Table with gratitude and humility. We stretch out empty hands to receive the bread and wine, for we have no offering to bring other than the offering God has provided **for us** in Jesus, the Lamb of God. We do not come to the Table professing our own faith or godliness, for we rely only upon the faith and obedience of Jesus for our salvation. We profess Christ only, for he is our true worship. Even in the Lord's Supper, we follow the spiritual principal set out by the apostle Paul: "I, yet not I but Christ" (Galatians 2:20).

Since we do not rely upon our own faith and obedience for salvation but only upon Jesus, we may come to the Table with *confidence* and thanksgiving, knowing that everything God requires is already given **for us** in Jesus. An old hymn says it well: "Nothing in my hands I bring. Simply to Thy cross I cling."

Jesus is always with us. Day by day, he is always close at hand, leading and guiding us through his Spirit, hearing our prayers and blessing us with his continual presence. In the Lord's Supper, we lift up our hearts to heaven, as the people who know Jesus as Lord, so that we may become more aware of his presence and enjoy his fellowship in a special way. When we take the bread and wine, we are lifted up in the communion of the Spirit to enjoy intimate fellowship with Christ.

Response

The Lord's Supper is a beautiful portrayal of the "wonderful exchange," where Jesus takes our poverty and gives us his riches. In the

> **Jesus feeds us in the bread and wine. He gives strength to our spirits, so that we may do his Kingdom work.**

Lord's Supper, Jesus gives himself to us, feeding us in the bread and wine (juice), nourishing our spirits and giving us strength to follow him. In turn, we **respond** to Jesus' self-giving in faith, obedience and thanksgiving, offering ourselves to God in Jesus' name as living sacrifices, which is our "true worship" (Romans 12:1).

The Lord's Supper is not a duty to perform so that God will be pleased with us. The Lord's Supper is not a ritual we do to appease God, so that he will not be angry with us. Rather, the Lord's Supper is a **celebration** of the salvation that is *already* ours in Jesus. The Lord's Supper should be a happy occasion. We take the bread and wine with joy and thanksgiving to remember the sacrifice Jesus made for our salvation. We participate, or share, in Jesus' fellowship with the Father, as the Holy Spirit lifts up our hearts into the presence of God. For this reason, many church traditions use the term, "**Holy Eucharist**," to refer to the Lord's Supper. **Eucharist** means "thanksgiving." We take the bread and wine with **thanksgiving** for the great love God shows us in Jesus. God sent his Son to show us how much he loves us (John 3:16). God showed his great love for us when Jesus died on the cross to take away the sin of the world (Romans 5:8). The Father and Son send the Holy Spirit to fill our hearts with love, so that we might love God and one another (Romans 5:5). Therefore, the Lord's Supper is a time of celebration. It is a **response** of joy and thanksgiving for God's love, goodness and mercy.

> "The body of our Lord Jesus Christ which was broken for you, keep your body and soul in eternal life. Take and eat this, in remembrance that Christ died for you, and feed on him in your hearts, by faith, with thanksgiving."—
> from *Our Modern Services*, Kenya

Discipleship: Living in Union with Christ

Summary

In the Lord's Supper, we remember the mighty act of deliverance two thousand years ago when Jesus set us free from the power of sin, death and the devil, just as the people of Israel remembered their deliverance from the bondage and slavery of Egypt. The same Jesus that delivered us then is with us *now* in the bread and wine, feeding us with his body and blood and giving us spiritual strength. In the Lord's Supper, we participate in the worship of heaven. The Holy Spirit lifts up our hearts into the presence of God, where Jesus includes us in his priestly offering to the Father. In the Lord's Supper, we respond with joy and thanksgiving to God's great love for us, as revealed in Jesus.

Pastors and church leaders are encouraged to make the Lord's Supper, or Holy Communion, a regular part of their worship services. Many churches celebrate the Lord's Supper weekly or monthly. When we take Holy Communion as the family of God, our Lord and Saviour **Jesus** Christ is present in a special way in the power of the Holy Spirit. Jesus feeds us in the bread and wine and gives us spiritual strength. The **Holy Spirit** lifts up our hearts to share in Jesus' fellowship with our **Father** in heaven. In the Lord's Supper, we share in the life, love and beauty of the Holy Trinity in a special way. To learn more about the "Last Supper" or "Holy Communion," read Mark 14:12-26; Luke 22:7-23, 1 Corinthians 11:22-26.

CHAPTER 5: DISCIPLESHIP (PART 2)

INTRODUCTION

The New Testament teaches us to live holy lives (1 Peter 1:15, 16). The word, "**holy**," means "set apart" for spiritual service. Believers are "set apart" from the world because we know God as "Abba, Father," and we serve Jesus as Lord. Our lives belong to Jesus. We are bought with a price (1 Corinthians 6:20). Jesus is our Master and Teacher. We are his disciples. We are his students and followers.

In the First Century, there were many teachers, or "rabbis." Each rabbi had disciples, or students, who lived with the teacher and followed him from village to village. A disciple served the teacher and helped to care for the teacher's needs. For example, a disciple might prepare food for the teacher when they were traveling. A disciple was not only a servant, however. A disciple was a **student**. A disciple learned from the teacher, so that he or she could become a teacher someday. But a disciple wanted more than knowledge. A disciple wanted to be like the teacher. A disciple wanted to become the kind of person the teacher was. For this reason, a disciple lived with the teacher and followed him everywhere. The disciple wanted to learn how the teacher thought, felt and acted in different circumstances in order to become like the teacher.

Jesus was a rabbi, or teacher. Like other rabbis of the time, Jesus had disciples. The disciples lived with Jesus. They were with him day and night. They followed him from village to village in order to learn to be like their Teacher and Master. Today, believers are Jesus' disciples. Like the twelve disciples of Jesus' day (Matthew 10:1-4), we are called to follow Jesus

Discipleship: Living in Union with Christ

(Matthew 4:18-20). We are called to learn from him, so that we can become more like him.

But how do we learn to become like Jesus? How do we "set apart" our lives for service to Jesus Christ? How do we become "holy" people? Is there a program we can follow or a series of steps to take that will make us holy? Must we buy the latest book to learn the secret to discipleship? Is discipleship a mystery that can be unlocked only with the key sold by a preacher on television?

HOLINESS

Many preachers in the United States describe discipleship as a difficult spiritual program that believers must strive to follow. For them, discipleship involves "effort," "perseverance" and "struggle." We must *strive* to be holy, they say. We must *humble* ourselves to be rid of pride. We must *examine* ourselves daily for signs of sin. We must *crucify* the flesh through regular fasting. In this view, we must **achieve** holiness by planning, prayer and hard work.

We grit our teeth, flex our spiritual muscles and stumble toward the finish line under our own steam.

Sadly, this common view of discipleship is a recipe for failure, because it focuses on our *personal* spiritual effort. In this view, we must strive to produce the fruit of repentance in our lives, for only

Many preachers describe discipleship as an exhausting spiritual program.

(Courtesy of themadnessofthemarathonblog.com)

then can we have assurance we are saved. This kind of teaching neglects the upward movement of grace (earth to heaven) in the priestly ministry of Jesus, because it lays the burden of discipleship upon *our* shoulders, not upon Jesus.

Discipleship, or Christian living, is not a burden that we must bear. Jesus said:

> **Matthew 11:28, 29:** "Come to me, all of you who are weary and carry heavy burdens, and I will give you rest. [29] Take my yoke upon you. Let me teach you, because I am humble and gentle at heart, and you will find **rest** for your souls. [30] For my yoke is **easy** to bear, and the burden I give you is **light**."

Jesus teaches us to take his "yoke," or "burden," upon our shoulders. His yoke is "easy" to bear. His burden is "light." Jesus' teaching is very different from the teaching of preachers who describe discipleship as "effort," "perseverance" and "struggle." God's commandments are not burdensome (1 John 5:3). Believers need not strive to achieve holiness by moral effort. To the contrary, we are **already** holy in the sight of God. The New Testament says:

> **Ephesians 1:3, 4:** All praise to God, the Father of our Lord Jesus Christ, who has blessed us with every spiritual blessing in the heavenly realms **because we are united with Christ.** [4] Even before he made the world, God loved us and chose us in Christ to be **holy** and without fault in his eyes.

> **Hebrews 10:10:** For God's will was for us to be made **holy** by the sacrifice of the body of Jesus Christ, once for all time.

> **Hebrews 10:14:** For by that one offering he forever made perfect those who are being made **holy**.

> **1 Peter 2:9:** But you are not like that, for you are a chosen people. You are royal priests, a **holy** nation, God's very own possession. As a result, you can show others the goodness of

God, for he called you out of the darkness into his wonderful light.

Ephesians 5:25-27: For husbands, this means love your wives, just as Christ loved the church. He gave up his life for her ²⁶ to make her **holy** and **clean**, **washed** by the cleansing of God's word. ²⁷ He did this to present her to himself as a glorious church without a spot or wrinkle or any other blemish. Instead, she will be **holy** and **without fault**.

Through **union with Christ** in the communion of the Spirit, believers are **holy** and **without fault** in the eyes of God. Holiness is not a spiritual quality that we slowly achieve through moral struggle and hard work. Holiness and "right-ness" before God are not spiritual qualities that we will receive in the distant future. Holiness and "right-ness" are ours *today* in union with Christ. The New Testaments says:

1 Corinthians 1:30: God has **united** you with Christ Jesus. For our benefit God made him to be wisdom itself. Christ made us **right** with God; he made us **pure** and **holy**, and he freed us from sin.

Jesus has made us "pure and holy." Jesus has freed us from the rule of sin (Romans 6:14). God "has blessed us with every spiritual blessing in the heavenly realms because we are **united with Christ**" (Ephesians 1:3). In union with Christ through the communion of the Spirit, all that belongs to Jesus belongs to us. Jesus has made us "right with God," so that we may share in his relationship with the Father.

Jesus did not save us from sin in order to give us a second chance at keeping the law. Jesus reconciled us to God so that we may enjoy communion ("relationship," fellowship") with our Father in heaven.

Hidden With Christ

> **Colossians 3:1-4:** Since you have been raised to new life with Christ, set your sights on the realities of heaven, where Christ sits in the place of honour at God's right hand. ² Think about the things of heaven, not the things of earth. ³ For you died to this life, and **your real life is hidden with Christ in God**. ⁴ And when Christ, who is your life, is revealed to the whole world, you will share in all his glory.

Despite the New Testament teaching that we are holy and without fault before God, we do not feel holy. If we are honest with ourselves, we know that often we act like sinners rather than saints. Despite the continuing presence of sin in our lives, however, the New Testament is clear that we are **saints**. In the life, death and resurrection of Jesus Christ, we are made "right" with God (2 Corinthians 5:21). In union with Christ through the communion of the Spirit, we are made "holy" in the eyes of God. We do not stand before God as sinners. We stand before God as **saints**. Yet, our "rightness" and holiness are **hidden with Christ** in God (Colossians 3:3). We will not see ourselves as we truly are until Jesus comes again. The New Testament says:

> **1 Corinthians 13:12:** Now we see things imperfectly, like puzzling reflections in a mirror, but then we will see everything with perfect clarity. All that I know now is partial and incomplete, but then I will know everything completely, just as God now knows me completely.

Today, we see ourselves imperfectly. We look into the mirror but we cannot see our true image. Our reflection is partial and incomplete. But God sees us completely. God sees us as the saints we are. God sees us as his beloved children, holy and "right" in his sight. The word, *apocalypse*, refers to the great **unveiling**, or "revelation," that will occur at the return of Christ, when all that is now hidden will be revealed. When

Discipleship: Living in Union with Christ

Christ is revealed, we will share in his glory (Colossians 3:4). Until that time, sin remains a presence in our lives, as we live "between the times" of the first and second coming of our Lord and Saviour Jesus Christ. In the eyes of the world, and even in our own eyes, believers look more like sinners than saints. But our lives are hidden with Christ. Our "right-ness" and holiness will be revealed only when Jesus comes again.

Because we are already holy and right in the eyes of God, we must learn to think of ourselves as "saints who sin" rather than as "miserable sinners" without worth. In God's sight, we are new creations in Christ. We are made "right" in Jesus (2 Corinthians 5:17, 21). Therefore, our beliefs about ourselves must be based on the truth of God rather than on human experience. In regard to holiness, we must focus on our identity as saints rather than on our earthly experience of sinfulness. The knowledge that we are God's children—holy, pure and without fault—gives us **dignity** and **worth**. We may hold our heads high, because we have been bought with a price, redeemed with the blood of Jesus and made holy in the communion of the Spirit (1 Corinthians 6:20; Ephesians 1:7; 1 Peter 1:18, 19; Hebrews 10:10). This is not arrogance, for we do not boast in ourselves, but in Jesus. Our holiness is not our own achievement. Our holiness is not a reward for the chosen few. Our holiness is a **participation** ("sharing") in the holiness of Jesus through the communion of the Spirit.

> We are not defined by sin.
>
> We are defined by our new identities in union with Christ.
>
> We are new creations in Christ.

> If we sons and daughters of God regard ourselves as lowly sinners who are unfit to approach our Father's throne, we make ourselves beggars, standing in a bread line for a hand out.

Sadly, many Christians have been taught to see themselves as "miserable sinners," who must approach the throne of grace with their heads down and their hats in their hands. This teaching focuses on our sin and unworthiness. It tries to make us feel guilty, afraid and ashamed. We may call this false teaching "worm theology," because it regards humans as lowly worms without worth. Preaching and teaching that makes us feel guilty, ashamed, unworthy and afraid is *not* the Gospel of Jesus Christ. We are not worms. We are saints! We are the beloved children of the King of the Universe. We are **glorious** and **beautiful**, because we share in the glory and beauty of our Lord Jesus.

> A man who knows he is a king will act like a king.
>
> A believer who knows she is a saint will act like a saint.

If we are taught to see ourselves as lowly worms without worth, we will *act* like lowly worms! Therefore, our identity as saints is the starting point for discipleship. **We must learn to see ourselves as saints in order to live holy lives**. Pastors and others who counsel believers must focus on the dignity and worth that belong to us in Jesus. Believers who were sexually abused, shamed or mistreated do not need to be told they are lowly worms. Believers who suffer from low self-esteem and feelings of shame and unworthiness desperately need to hear the good news that we are holy, right and beautiful in the eyes of God.

Some churches rightly teach that salvation is a gift to the sinner. Yet, they *wrongly* teach that holiness is a reward, or "second blessing," given only to the saintly few. There are two major problems with teaching a "second blessing." First, it divides the unity of the Holy Trinity by separating the work of the Son from the work of the Spirit. According to this teaching, our right standing with God is based on Jesus' sacrifice on the cross (which is correct). "Holiness," however, is a separate work of the Spirit given only to a few as a reward for saintly living (which is incorrect). The work of the Son and the work of the Spirit cannot be divided. Like our right standing before God given us through the sacrifice of Christ on the cross, holiness is also given to us freely by grace through the wonderful exchange, where we receive *all* Christ's riches. In the "wonderful exchange," we do not receive only a "part" of Jesus. We receive the "whole Christ." Secondly, the teaching of a "second blessing" is contrary to the good news that salvation is "all of grace," not reward.

Become What You Are

Discipleship is not a slow, gradual struggle to achieve holiness. There is nothing we can do to make ourselves more holy, for we are *already* holy in the sight of God. Discipleship is about discovering our identity as saints and learning to live accordingly. In other words, Jesus calls us to **become who we are**.

But how do we become who we are? How do we learn to live as the saints we already are? We find the answer in Jesus' story about the Vine and the branches. Jesus said:

> **John 15:1-5 ERV:** "I am the true vine, and my Father is the gardener. ² He cuts off every branch of mine that does not produce fruit. He also trims every branch that produces fruit to prepare it to produce even more. ³ You have already been prepared to produce more fruit by the teaching I have given you. ⁴ Stay joined to me and I will stay joined to you. No branch can produce fruit alone. It must stay connected to

the vine. It is the same with you. **You cannot produce fruit alone. You must stay joined to me**. ⁵ I am the vine, and you are the branches. **If you stay joined to me, and I to you, you will produce plenty of fruit**. But separated from me you will not be able to do anything."

Jesus offers the perfect description of **discipleship** as "**living in union with Christ**." Jesus is the Vine. Believers are the branches. The branches depend totally upon the Vine for their life and nourishment. The Vine provides everything the branches need to live and to bear fruit. Apart from the Vine, the branches can do nothing. In union with the Vine, however, the branches produce "plenty of fruit."

Jesus is the Vine.
We are the branches.
(Courtesy of Pinterest.com)

"Holiness," or Christian living, is the fruit of union with Christ in the communion of the Spirit. We bear the fruit of holiness because we are "in" the Vine. The burden of bearing fruit rests on the Vine, *not* on the branches. Instead of struggle, perseverance and effort, we **rest** in the presence of Jesus, who lives in us through the indwelling of the Holy Spirit. Like branches joined to the Vine, we receive the spiritual nourishment and strength we need to live as his disciples. By staying joined to the True Vine, we bear the fruit of Christian living. In union with Christ through the communion of the Spirit, we receive the strength to live out the reality of our *new humanity* in him. In short, we become who we are by staying **joined to the Vine.**

Discipleship: Living in Union with Christ

Discipleship means to **abide** in Jesus. We abide in Jesus by spending time with him in prayer and Bible study. We abide in Jesus by worshipping with other believers and feeding on the body and blood of Christ in the Lord's Supper. We abide in Jesus through sacred dance and songs of praise and thanksgiving. We abide in Jesus through meditation or in quiet walks by the sea or in quiet prayer in the noisy traffic of the city. We abide with Jesus whenever and wherever we are aware of his continual presence in our lives. We abide in Jesus whenever we lift up our hearts in praise and thanksgiving for his great love for us. As we abide in Jesus, we **receive** everything we need for discipleship, or Christian living. As the branches receive all they need from the Vine in order to bear fruit, we receive all we need for discipleship in union with Christ through the communion of the Holy Spirit.

> **Christian living is not a struggle to become "more and more" holy.**
>
> **Christian living is receiving "again and again," by faith, the holiness that is already ours in Jesus.**

Set Free in Jesus

Before we were baptised, before we made a "personal decision" for Christ, even before the world was made, God chose us to be holy and without fault in union with Christ (Ephesians 1:3, 4). The knowledge that we are already holy "in Christ" **sets us free** from the impossible task of making ourselves holy through moral effort or religious works. In union with Christ through the communion of the Spirit, we are set free to become who we are. Through the power of the Holy Spirit, we are set free to live as saints.

Therefore, Christian living is not a matter of effort, perseverance and struggle. Holiness is not a spiritual quality that comes to us "more and more" through moral effort or religious works. To the contrary, holiness comes to us "again and again" by grace through faith, as we "keep our eyes on Jesus" (Hebrews 12:2), receiving anew each day the riches that are fully ours in union with Christ. Therefore, we may **rest** in all that Jesus has done **for us**, as we await the day when all that is now hidden will be fully revealed.

We do not become "more and more" holy with the passing of time. There is nothing we can do to make ourselves more holy. We are *already* holy in union with Christ. The passing of time serves to unveil the holiness that is already ours in Jesus.

EVANGELISM

The Christian Church is a body of believers gathered by the Holy Spirit in faith, built up in love and sent into the world with a message of hope. The message of hope we take to the world is a message of **reconciliation**. The New Testament says:

> **1 Corinthians 5:19-21:** For God was in Christ, **reconciling** the world to himself, no longer counting people's sins against them. And he gave us this wonderful **message of reconciliation**. [20] So we are Christ's ambassadors; God is making his appeal through us. We speak for Christ when we plead, "Come back to God!" [21] For God made Christ, who never sinned, to be the offering for our sin, so that we could be made right with God through Christ.

The message of **reconciliation** is the starting point for evangelism. The evangelist proclaims to unbelievers the good news that **everyone** is "made right" with God through Christ. When Jesus took our sinful humanity from his mother Mary, he healed it and restored it to right relationship with God. Because we live and move and exist in Jesus, everyone is included in his reconciling life, death and resurrection. We must be very clear about this! **All humanity** is reconciled to God in Jesus (2 Corinthians 5:19; Colossians 1:20). All humanity is "made right" with God in Jesus (Romans 5:16, 19; 1 Corinthians 1:30; 2 Corinthians 5:21). The Father's love is universal (John 3:16). No one is excluded from the love of God revealed in Jesus Christ. God loves all his children. The evangelist announces the message of reconciliation to unbelievers and calls them to "come back to God" (2 Corinthians 5:20).

When we take the good news of Jesus Christ to our families, neighbours, communities and nations, there are certain things to remember:

- God loves the world (John 3:16).
- God sent his Son to save the world (John 3:16, 17).
  - Jesus Christ has taken away the sin of the world (John 1:29).
  - Everyone is forgiven and reconciled to God in Jesus (Col 1:19, 20; 2 Cor 5:19).
  - God does not want anyone to perish (2 Peter 3:9)
  - Jesus calls everyone to repent and follow his way of love (Mark 1:14, 15).
- Jesus is preparing a place for us in his Father's house (John 14:2).

Therefore, we proclaim the good news of reconciliation **first**. *After* we have proclaimed the good news of reconciliation, we summon unbelievers to **faith** and **repentance** with the certain knowledge that **God loves them**.

We must be careful, however, to call unbelievers to faith and repentance in a way that honours Jesus Christ. Many evangelists lay the burden for salvation upon the sinner. The evangelist announces, "This is what Jesus Christ has done for you, but you will not be saved *unless* you make your own personal decision for Christ as your Saviour." Or, the evangelist may say, "Jesus Christ loved you and gave his life for you on the Cross, but you will be saved only *if* you give your heart to him." This incorrect form of preaching makes the Gospel sound like a business deal: "**If** you repent, **then** God will be gracious." "**If** you have faith, **then** God will save you." "**If** you obey, **then** you will go to heaven." This form of evangelism does not honour Jesus Christ because it lays the burden of faith and repentance upon the sinner, not upon Jesus. In this form of preaching, God's grace and goodness appear to depend upon the sinner's faith and repentance. In other words, the "business deal" is not closed until the sinner does his part. In this view, the sinner cannot be certain of his standing with God because his salvation finally depends upon his own imperfect faith, repentance and obedience. This kind of preaching causes doubt, fear and lack of assurance.

Reconciliation, however, is not a business deal. There are no conditions we must meet in order to be reconciled to God. Reconciliation is "all of grace." It is **unconditional**. In Jesus, God freely and lovingly provides all that is required for our salvation. We are saved by the perfect faith and obedience that Jesus offers to the Father **in our name**. We must proclaim the good news to unbelievers that they may trust **Jesus' response** on their behalf and in their name. The message of universal reconciliation brings joy, peace and assurance to those who turn to Jesus.

When proclaiming the Gospel, the evangelist must give central place to Jesus. He or she must boldly and clearly proclaim the good news that Jesus has provided the full, perfect, **all-sufficient** response to God **in our place** and in our name. In proclaiming the good news of Jesus Christ, the evangelist may say:

> (Evangelist): "God loves you so deeply and so completely that he has given himself for you in Jesus, his beloved Son.

Discipleship: Living in Union with Christ

In Jesus, God has claimed you as his own. Long before you ever believed in him, Jesus believed for you. Jesus obeyed God for you and on your behalf. Jesus professed perfect faith to God for you and in your name. Jesus offered perfect obedience to the Father for you and in your name. Everything needed for your salvation is *already* done for you in Jesus. He claims you as his own and presents you to the Father as one who has *already* believed through him, who has *already* obeyed through him, and who is *already* accepted by the Father in him. Therefore, renounce yourself, take up your cross and follow Jesus!"[2]

True "Gospel preaching" focuses on the good news of what God has done for **everyone** in Jesus. Preaching the Gospel this way frees us from doubt about our own faith, repentance and obedience, for we do not depend upon our personal spiritual experiences—we depend upon Jesus. Preaching the Gospel this way sets us free from fear, for we are assured of God's love for us, as revealed in Jesus. Because we depend entirely upon Jesus for our salvation, we are set free from doubt and fear. We are set free to respond to the Gospel in joyful worship, praise and thanksgiving.

Therefore, we call sinners to faith and repentance **because God loves them**. Repentance and faith are not conditions for God's love. They are **responses** to God's love! God is calling his children home, so that they may live in his love and share it with others. This is the good news we are called to proclaim. This is evangelism that honours Jesus.

We do not repent and believe in order to be saved. We repent and believe because we *are* saved.

---

[2] Adapted from the writings of T.F. Torrance.

The Logic of Grace

Salvation is "all of grace." Everything that God requires for our salvation is freely and graciously given to us in Jesus. Nothing remains for us to do to earn our salvation. "All of grace," however, does not mean "nothing of man." In other words, the free and complete gift of salvation through Jesus does not mean that our response to the Gospel is unimportant or unnecessary. Jesus commands us to repent and believe the Gospel (Mark 1:15). Jesus commands us to love one another (John 13:34). Jesus commands us to take up our crosses and follow him (Matthew 16:24). But we can only respond to Jesus' commands because he has already offered perfect faith and obedience to the Father **for us**. Our imperfect response to God's commands is supported and made possible by Jesus' perfect response to the Father **in our place** and in our name. Jesus takes our imperfect responses of faith and obedience, gathers them up with his own perfect response and presents them to the Father in our name. Apart from Jesus, we can do nothing (John 15:5). Without the prior perfect response of Jesus, our imperfect responses to God would fall far short of the mark. Yet, our inadequate, imperfect responses are pleasing and acceptable to God, because they are gathered up and **included** in Jesus' perfect response to the Father.

Our personal acts of faith and obedience are no less real, however, because they are gathered up into Jesus' perfect response of faith and obedience. In order to understand how our imperfect responses fit into Jesus' perfect response offered to the Father in our name, we must think deeply about the incarnation of Jesus Christ. The man we know as Jesus of Nazareth is both fully human and fully divine. Jesus is the Eternal Word of God, who was with God in the beginning, and he is God (John 1:1-3). The Eternal Word of

Discipleship: Living in Union with Christ

God came down from heaven and became a human being (John 1:14) and was given the name "Jesus" (Matthew 1:21; Luke 1:31). Jesus was conceived by the Holy Spirit in the womb of the Virgin Mary (Matthew 1:18; Luke 1:35). Therefore, Jesus is the fully divine "Son of God." Apart from the incarnation, there would be no person called Jesus of Nazareth. In other words, apart from a divine act of God, the man we know as Jesus would not exist. At the same time, Jesus was "born of a woman" (Galatians 4:4). He came forth from the womb of the Virgin Mary "in a body like the bodies we sinners have" (Romans 8:3). He was born as a human being (Philippians 2:7). The fact that Jesus is **fully divine** does not diminish his humanity in any way. Jesus is **fully human**, just as we are.

Therefore, the words and acts of Jesus are **both** fully divine and fully human. Because Jesus is divine, his human words carry the authority of God. Because Jesus is human, his divine word comes to us in ordinary human language, so that we can understand. The divinity, or "God-ness," of Jesus does not diminish his human words and deeds. The words and deeds of Jesus are no less human because he is divine.

In a similar way, Jesus' perfect response to the Father in our name does not diminish our personal response to God. Just as the human response of Jesus is not less real because he is divine, our human responses to God are not less real because they are joined to Jesus' perfect response. Jesus' perfect response to the Father in our name does not make our personal response unimportant or unnecessary. To the contrary, our human response to God is made possible because it is joined to Jesus' response to God through the communion of the Spirit. Divine agency does not exclude human participation. Rather, divine agency *enables* our human response to grace. Apart from Jesus, we have nothing to offer God. In union with Christ through the communion of the Spirit, however, our offering of praise and thanksgiving is fully pleasing and acceptable to our heavenly Father. Therefore, "all of grace" means "all of man."

In summary, God provides everything needed for our salvation in Jesus. At the same time Jesus calls us to respond to God's goodness by faith, repentance and obedience. Our personal faith, repentance and obedience, however, are not conditions for grace. They are the appropriate **responses** to grace. Jesus' perfect response of faith and obedience to the Father in our name does not make our personal responses to grace unimportant or unnecessary. To the contrary, Jesus enables our responses of faith, repentance and obedience by gathering them up in his priestly offering and presenting them to the Father in our name.

> **Colossians 2:6, 7:** And now, just as you accepted Christ Jesus as your Lord, you must continue to follow him. 7 Let your roots grow down into him, and let your lives be built on him. Then your faith will grow strong in the truth you were taught, and you will overflow with thankfulness.

CHAPTER 5: SUMMARY

In Jesus Christ, we live and move and exist. Jesus Christ is the Creator and Sustainer of the Universe. All things are created through Jesus. Jesus holds the universe together and sustains it with his power. In the incarnation of Jesus Christ, when the eternal Son of God united himself to sinful flesh in the womb of the Virgin Mary, God established an unbreakable union with humanity in Jesus.

Jesus is the Vine, we are the branches. He is the Temple, we are stones in the Temple. Our close personal relationship with Jesus is called "union with Christ." In union with Christ, all that belongs to Jesus becomes ours in a "wonderful exchange," where Jesus takes our poverty and gives us his riches. In the "wonderful exchange," Jesus takes our sinfulness and "wrong-ness" and gives us his holiness and "right-ness." In the "wonderful exchange," all humanity is reconciled to God.

The "wonderful exchange" does not happen in only a single moment of time. Jesus took our sinful humanity from the Virgin Mary and healed and cleansed it throughout every stage of human life. Jesus re-lived the life of Adam. Unlike Adam, however, Jesus offered perfect faith and obedience to the Father in our place and in our name. Therefore, we are no longer "in Adam" and under the power of sin, death and the devil. We are "in Jesus." We are set free from the power of sin, death and the devil. We are no longer stained by Adam's sin. Jesus healed and cleansed our sinful humanity and made it new. We are new creations in Christ.

Jesus is our High Priest. In a movement of grace from heaven to earth and back again from earth to heaven, Jesus represents the Father to us *and* Jesus represents us to the Father. As the divine Son of God, Jesus speaks the word of

God **to us**. As the human son of Mary, Jesus responds to the word of God **for us**. Because we live and move and exist in Jesus, all humanity is included in Jesus' priestly offering of perfect faith and obedience to the Father. Everything needed for our salvation is freely and graciously given to us in Jesus. Jesus puts an end to religion. In Jesus, God provides all he requires.

Everything Jesus does **for us** is made real **in us** by the ministry of the Holy Spirit. In the communion ("fellowship") of the Holy Spirit, believers actively, knowingly, willingly, thankfully participate ("share") in our union with Christ. The riches and blessings we receive from Jesus in the "wonderful exchange" are "personalised," or made real in us by the Spirit. By the Spirit, the perfect faith and obedience that Jesus offered to the Father for us takes root in us.

Union with Christ is an "identity-forming" relationship. When the Eternal Word of God united himself to humanity in the womb of the Virgin Mary, he began to cleanse and heal our sinful flesh in order to make it new. Throughout his life on earth, the Son of God re-made and re-shaped sinful humanity. Jesus gave us new "identities." In Jesus, we are new creations. Through the communion of the Holy Spirit, our new identities in union with Christ are made real and active **in us**. Union with Christ through the communion of the Spirit moulds and shapes us at the deepest levels of our being, where our lives are hidden with Christ in God. **Discipleship** is the process of **discovering** our new identities in Jesus.

In this manual, we explored discipleship in relation to faith, worship, prayer, the sacraments, godly living ("holiness") and evangelism. *Faith* is an important part of discipleship. By faith, we personally receive the blessings that are ours in union with Christ. Yet, even more important than our own

Discipleship: Living in Union with Christ

personal faith "in" Jesus is the faith **of** Jesus, who offers his perfect faith to the Father **in our place** and in our name. Our right standing with God does not depend upon our "personal" faith. It depends upon the faithfulness of God as embodied in Jesus. Jesus is the Leader of our faith. Jesus makes our faith complete. Our right standing with God is grounded in, and supported by, the faith of Jesus.

Worship is an important part of discipleship, or Christian living. Worship is our response of praise and thanksgiving to God for all he has done for us in Jesus. In worship, we enjoy communion with God. In worship, the community of faith is lifted up by the Holy Spirit into the loving heart of the Holy Trinity, where we share in the Son's fellowship with the Father. True Christian worship is "Christ-centred," for only Jesus has the authority to enter the Most Holy Place in heaven. Christ-centred worship is participating, or "sharing," in Jesus' High-Priestly ministry in the communion of the Holy Spirit.

Like worship, prayer is an important part of discipleship. Through prayer, we nurture our relationship with our Father in heaven. When we do not know how to pray, Jesus prays for us. In the "wonderful exchange," Jesus gathers up our imperfect prayers, cleanses them, and includes them with his own prayers, so that they rise together as a single fragrant offering to our Father in heaven. As in worship, prayer is "all of grace," for Jesus our High Priest is at the Father's side, speaking on our behalf

God graciously gives us the sacraments of baptism and the Lord's Supper as proper ways to respond to God's love and goodness toward us, as revealed in Jesus. Through the sacraments of baptism and the Lord's Supper, we **participate**, or share, in Jesus's priestly offering of perfect faith and obedience to God. Baptism is a public sign of our once-and-for-all union with Christ through the communion of the Spirit. In the Lord's Supper, we are continually fed spiritually through our union with Christ. Both sacraments remind us that we find our lives outside ourselves in union with Christ through the communion of the Spirit.

The "one baptism" of the New Testament refers primarily to Jesus' baptism **for us**. Jesus was baptised in our place, on our behalf and in our name. By receiving John's baptism, Jesus identifies with sinners. Jesus puts himself in the place of sinners. Jesus bears our guilt and submits to God's judgement **for us**. As our High Priest, Jesus receives the baptism of the Spirit in his humanity in the name of all humanity, so that the Holy Spirit can be poured out on everyone. Today, Jesus continues to baptise believers with the Holy Spirit (Luke 3:16). Jesus sends the Spirit so that we may know and enjoy our union with him. Jesus sends the "Spirit of adoption," so that we may enter into Jesus' "family-fellowship" with the Father. Through the baptism of the Spirit, we know God as "Abba, Father."

Like baptism, the Lord's Supper, or Holy Communion, is a sign that points to Jesus. In the Lord's Supper, we **remember** the sacrifice Jesus made to take away the sin of the world. In the Lord's Supper, we **participate** ("share") in Jesus's priestly offering of perfect faith and obedience to God. In the Lord's Supper, we **respond** to God's love and goodness for us, as revealed in Jesus. When we celebrate the Lord's Supper, Jesus is present with us in the communion of the Spirit. Jesus feeds our spirits in the bread and wine and draws us into his fellowship with the Father.

Disciples of Jesus Christ are "holy." We are "set apart" to serve God and others. Holiness, however, is not a spiritual quality we strive to achieve by moral effort, perseverance and struggle. We are made holy by the sacrifice of Jesus Christ.

Discipleship: Living in Union with Christ

In union with Christ through the communion of the Spirit, we are holy and without fault in the eyes of God. We are saints with dignity and worth, because we are bought with the precious blood of Jesus. Our holiness is a **participation** ("sharing") in the holiness of Jesus through the communion of the Spirit. Yet, our holiness is hidden with Christ in God until Jesus returns to unveil all that is now hidden.

Discipleship is about discovering our identity as saints and learning to live accordingly. We "become who we are" by abiding in Jesus. As branches receive all they need from the Vine in order to bear fruit, we receive all we need for discipleship from Jesus. In union with Christ through the communion of the Spirit, we **rest** in all that Jesus does for us, as we await the day when all that is now hidden will be fully revealed.

Through evangelism, the Church proclaims the good news about Jesus. The starting point for evangelism is the message of reconciliation. The evangelist proclaims to unbelievers the good news that **everyone** is "made right" with God through Christ. We call sinners to faith and repentance because God loves them. Through evangelism, God is calling his children home. The Church may confidently proclaim the good news that everything needed for the salvation of the world is provided for us in Jesus. **Amen.**

Manufactured by Amazon.ca
Bolton, ON

27443519R00058